To Dad Cornwell , Christmas 1987
from: Randy + Wray Jean.
            Cornwell

BECOMING

Books by Blaine M. Yorgason and/or Brenton G. Yorgason

Becoming
The Shadow Taker**
The Loftier Way: Tales from the Ancient American Frontier
Brother Brigham's Gold
Ride the Laughing Wind
The Miracle
Chester, I Love You
Double Exposure
Seeker of the Gentle Heart
The Krystal Promise
A Town Called Charity and Other Stories about Decisions
The Bishop's Horse Race
The Courage Covenant (Massacre at Salt Creek)
Windwalker (movie version—out of print)
The Windwalker
Others
Charlie's Monument
From First Date to Chosen Mate
Tall Timber (out of print)
Miracles and the Latter-day Saint Teenager (out of print)
From Two to One*
From This Day Forth* (out of print)
Creating a Celestial Marriage* (textbook)
Marriage and Family Stewardships* (textbook)

Tapes

Caring and Sharing (Blaine M. Yorgason—two taped talks)
Things Most Plain and Precious (Brenton G. Yorgason—two taped talks)
The Joyous Way (Blaine M. Yorgason—two taped talks)
The Miracle (dramatized tape of book)
Charlie's Monument (taped reading of book)
The Bishop's Horse Race (taped reading of book)

*Coauthored with Wesley R. Burr and Terry R. Baker
**Coauthored with Carl J. Eaton

BECOMING

Blaine M. Yorgason
Brenton G. Yorgason

Deseret Book Company
Salt Lake City, Utah

©1986 Deseret Book Company
All rights reserved
Printed in the United States of America

No part of this book may be reproduced in any
form or by any means without permission in writing
from the publisher, Deseret Book Company,
P.O. Box 30178, Salt Lake City, Utah 84130

ISBN 0-87579-034-8
Library of Congress Catalog Card Number 86-70295

First printing March 1986
Second printing September 1986

For our brothers and sisters

Marilynn
Gary
Judy
Valerie
Gregory

You are great!

CONTENTS

CONTRIBUTORS

The accounts that follow, shared with us by the people below and a few others who wished their names to be withheld, are, so far as we know, true. Most have been somewhat edited, due primarily to space considerations or to eliminate very personal thoughts and feelings. Then, too, editing has been used occasionally to correct spelling and grammar. In all cases, we have done our best to preserve the original intentions and messages of the contributors.

Ellen Fagg
Jodie Ellis
Nancy Cleveland
Cynthia Passey
Randall Stucki
Marcia Petterborg
Lorena Jones
Carin Green
Blaine Hales
David Anderson
Shawna Hallett
Suzanne Adams
Tricia Tingey
Cindy Webster
Allyson Amann

Sherri Lloyd
Steve Chipman
DeWayne Erdmann
Debbie Rupp
Laura Newman
Sabrina Vanderhoof
Colleen McKinlay
Max Gardner
Jennie Barnes
Jeff Anderson
Kevin Beckstrom
Ilene Sandholtz
Susan Eliza Tintle
Russell O. Cahoon
Stan Manley

Lori Flaman
Bob Murri
Cindy Hooper
Lila Rector
Crystal Heer
Jamie Cram
Nadine MacKinnon
Tracey Evans
Robert Stevens
Tami Lloyd
Deann DeBate
Becky Jones
Michelle Radford
Laurie Pratt
Michael J. Syme

Cindy Wilmshurst	Gayla Black	Debra Johnson
Kaye Larson	Debbie Buchanan	Gary R. Blodgett
Paul Horstmeier	Susan Savage	Susan Galloway
Sharon Mustard	Vickie Walton	Cheri Weight
Len Ellis		

It would have been our preference to include the names of these people with their accounts, but almost every one asked to remain anonymous. We of course complied, knowing that what is shared in secret, the Lord is more able to reward openly. Our prayer is that the Lord will bless them for their acts of charity.

THE SON

This evening, very briefly,
I sat in silent solitude
and watched with fascinated awe
the setting of the sun.

I saw first its quiet beauty,
and I knew that it had shown
so that I, and others with me,
might see all that beauty is.

For a moment then I closed my eyes
and felt with pleasured peace
the warming of the sun's last rays,
its gift, with light, to me.

Pausing suddenly I listened
as my mind began to stir—
telling me of things not known
about the sun and me.

I thought of my dependence,
the light I use, and warmth;
and how my world is set on course,
revolving without my choice.

And then I made that quantum leap—
to see, to feel, to know
that what I truly saw tonight
was not the source itself—

But was, as I, responding—
commanded and complying,
fulfilling now its destiny,
a constant, ever giving.

I wondered, as the darkness spread,
of the true Source . . . I had not seen.
The Son my mind saw clearly now,
and what He did for me:

The Garden and the drops of blood,
the cross on which He hung,
the price He paid to light my life,
the suffering that He bore.

And now his warmth and shining glow,
much more than the sun above,
radiates out so powerfully
with wondrous light and love.

To set on course my own small life,
with purpose to go forth,
and share with constancy and love—
His light with everyone.

Brenton G. Yorgason

THE "CARRIER AND BARRIER" PRINCIPLE

When the two of us were a great deal younger, our father staked a claim on a mine high in the mountains of Sanpete County, Utah. We brothers got involved, and we all had high hopes of drawing out of the earth an ore that at the time was used in manufacturing steel. Ultimately the mine did not work, but we certainly did, spending backbreaking days with each other and with Dad.

During one of our frequent "breaks," we chanced upon a brilliant, sparkling, golden substance near the mine's entrance. In our youthful exuberance, we proclaimed to Dad that we had struck gold and were thus too rich to continue working.

Dad took the glittering ore into his hand, leaned against the support beam he was building, and, wiping his brow, said simply, "What you have looks like gold, boys, but it doesn't weigh like gold. It's nothing more than iron pyrite—fool's gold. Test the weight, and you can always tell."

In frustration, our brother Gary took the rock and threw it out and down the mountain. "Splunk!" Far below us the rock dropped into the center of a quiet beaver pond. Then the rock was gone. Almost instantly the splash disappeared too, and after that there were only the ripples, spreading outward toward the edge of the pond.

"Bet you almost killed some poor beaver," Brent volunteered. "Maybe now he'll float to the top."

We continued to watch, seeing if something else would happen, and Dad took that moment of mountain stillness to teach.

"Each of you is like that rock," he said quietly.

"You mean bright and shiny?" Blaine asked hopefully.

"Not quite." Dad smiled.

"Shucks!"

"Hey, do you want to be fool's gold?" Dad asked.

"No! I mean—"

"Blaine, no human being is fool's gold. We are every one the genuine article, a literal son or daughter of God. That's why I am always telling you to treat people with care."

"So what does that have to do with that rock?"

"Mostly nothing. Actually, what I had in mind was the splash, and that has everything to do with people. Each of you will make splashes as you go through life. Every time you do something, that will be a splash, and always the water will make you wet. You won't even be able to help it. You do something, and you will be affected by it."

"Like what?" Brent asked.

"Well, like school. The more education you get, the more you will know about what you have studied. And the more you know, the more valuable you will be to those who are willing to pay for your knowledge."

"People pay for knowledge?" Blaine asked.

"Of course they do. That's called having a job. For instance, you know how to backwash Culligan tanks, so I am willing to hire you to backwash at my Culligan plant."

"Which reminds me," Gary said, grinning. "I was supposed to be paid the middle of last month—"

Dad popped Gary on the shoulder with his fist, the two tussled for a moment, and then, with Gary pinned and groaning, Dad got serious again.

"The other parts of the splash you need to consider are the ripples. Just as that rock made ripples go out and out, everything you ever do will send out ripples too. Always people will be affected by what you do."

"Like how?" Gary asked quietly as he rubbed his shoulder.

"Like your friend in town who got arrested the other night stealing gas," Dad stated quietly.

Gary's eyes opened wide. "You know about that?"

"Of course I do. Because of my Church position, the ripples washed over me. Now, who else do you think was affected by that boy's splash?"

"His family," Gary answered quickly.

"Absolutely. So was the policeman who had to arrest him and who is a close friend of the boy's father; so were his friends at school, which includes you—"

"Hey, he wasn't *that* good of a friend!"

"See," Dad said with a smile, "you're already being affected. Two months ago he was the greatest guy you knew. Right?"

Gary quietly nodded, and Dad went on. "The thing I want you all to remember is that because your ripples affect others, and because you were the cause of those ripples, you will be held accountable for them. Whatever we do to other people, however we make them feel, God holds us accountable for that. So always try to make your splashes clean, and your ripples good."

"Yeah," Brent said, "like VonRay Warner, who has been teaching Blaine how to build radios and model airplanes."

"Exactly," Dad responded. "VonRay is older than Blaine. Think how easy it would have been for him to make Blaine feel foolish. Because he didn't, he'll be blessed."

Well, the conversation continued, and all these years later, it is still remembered. We all make splashes and ripples in life, affecting both ourselves and others, and those are the substance of mortality from which we will be judged.

In the scriptures we find two diametrically opposed themes that we will examine carefully in this volume. The prophet Lehi expressed them most clearly when he declared, first, that the plan of God is that *"men are, that they might have joy,"* and, second, that Satan *"seeketh that all men might be miserable like unto himself."* (2 Nephi 2:25, 27.) Since Christ "came into the world to do the will of [his] Father," (3 Nephi 27:13), it follows that Christ too seeks the joy of all mankind.

To be true disciples of God and Jesus Christ, then, it becomes apparent that we must constantly do two things. First, we must stand as a barrier against misery in all of its ugly forms, no matter *where* it is found; in other words, we must not send out ripples of pain. And second, we must be a carrier of joy to all children of God everywhere, no matter *who* they are; in other words, the ripples we send out must be for good.

In the accounts that follow, we hope to show the effects of doing or not doing these two things, and thus help to give you a clearer picture of how to become a true disciple of Jesus Christ in the world today.

CHAPTER ONE

KINDNESS BEGETS KINDNESS

My family has always been an emotional pillar of strength to me. I always knew, even during my teen years, that no matter what else happened—if my closest friend betrayed me, if my dog died, or even if I flunked algebra—no matter what happened, I could turn to my parents and my brothers and sisters and they would support me. They loved me, and they made me feel like I was a one-of-a-kind special person. That has been the case ever since I can remember. But somehow, during my senior year in high school, I began to take that love and concern for granted. And then, thankfully, I learned.

I came home late one Saturday night from a date. I was tired and more than just a little grouchy. All I wanted to do was splash my face with a little water and crawl into bed. As I lumbered up the stairs to my room, I suddenly remembered the last thing my mother had told me before I had dashed out the door five hours before: "Ellen, make sure you get your sheets and make up your bed before you go. And did you get your room picked up?"

As I was prone to do, I had, well, not really ignored her, but rather had sort of disregarded her advice. Thus, in my present state of mind, I was

1

suddenly faced with the unpleasant prospect of searching out my sheets and making my bed, a terrible delay of my much-craved sleep.

I had not cleaned my room, and in my exhausted state I absently considered the strategically placed piles of clothing that I knew would be on the floor and slowly stumbled toward the bed. Suddenly I noticed that there were no piles of once-worn clothes, and the bed, my bed, was *made*, with the sheets carefully straight, the blankets tucked in, and the sheets invitingly turned down. The window was open, just enough to let a cool breeze drift in, and there on my pillow was a loving note from my mother.

Suddenly I was brought to my senses. I felt guilty for being so slothful and ungrateful. What kind of selfish person was I that I couldn't even take care of my own room, my own bed? I thought of all the pressures on my mother, and yet my actions made her still have to take care of me, her almost-grown-up daughter. I knew she had probably been hurt when she had seen my messy room. But instead of taking one look at it, throwing the sheets into a pile, and crying, "Clean up and grow up!" she had closed her eyes to the mess, carefully stepped through my clutter, and lovingly spent the evening cleaning my room.

A wave of love washed over me, and I silently vowed that I would become the person she had so patiently taught me to be. Dropping to my knees, I thanked Heavenly Father for my sweet mother, and then I quickly climbed into bed and was enveloped between a set of fresh-smelling sheets and my mother's all-encompassing love.

Now lean back for a moment, close your eyes, take a deep breath, and *think* about what you have just read about disciple-ship. There are two individuals in this story, a mother and a daughter. The mother has obviously learned much about dis-

2

cipleship, while the daughter still has a way to go. The exciting benefit from this experience is that the daughter, receiving and then learning from her mother's love, is now moving in the direction of true discipleship.

Perhaps this would be an appropriate place to share with you a law of human nature—a law that is true but that is something we rarely stop to consider. This law was articulated by a man named Deutch, and thus it is called Deutch's Law. It states simply that *the more we act in certain ways, the more others around us will act in those same ways.* If we were to apply this law to love, we could say that *the more we act in loving ways, the more others around us will act in loving ways— both toward us as well as toward others.* It is really a natural and positive restatement of the golden rule.

To reinforce how spontaneously this law works, let us now drop in on another incident and consider the effects of loving acts upon a friend of ours.

> Caring, to me, is inseparably connected with sacrifice; and sacrifice, in turn, goes hand in hand with love. My mother and father exhibit such qualities so completely and so continually; how can I take any one incident out of context and explain that the incident is how I learned about caring.
>
> My mother is always up to her neck in things to do, places to go, people to speak to, and business to attend to. She writes books, runs a household, and finances her children through their schooling and early years of marriage. Yet she still finds time to visit her daughters and sons, married and living many hundreds of miles away. She cleans their homes from top to bottom, washes out cupboards and closets, scrubs and waxes the floors, cleans the carpets and curtains, refinishes couches and chairs, babysits the kids, cooks huge meals, and then fills our pocketbooks with fresh greenery as she leaves, all for no reason but love. And this is not all.

Whenever a grandchild is born (when it is economically feasible, and often when it isn't), Mother flies down to the daughter or daughter-in-law who is bearing, and she goes through the same routine mentioned above. Nor does this mention the tender loving care, sympathy, comfort, and encouragement a daughter needs from her mother at such times. Such sacrifice and constant service to her children is so fervently extended from our mother, yet she never expects a *thing* in return, *never*!

She would gladly give up a pork chop, or roll, or portion of corn, or whatever it might be, so that someone else might have seconds. I remember when she would so quickly buy me a new dress for a prom and forfeit buying a badly needed item at home, or bypass a repair on a dishwasher or oven. Whatever surplus money she may earn on a book goes directly into the purchase of a new refrigerator or dryer for a married daughter, or for a down payment on a house for a son going through law school. Mother and Father even bought the diamond for one future son-in-law so that he could become engaged to their daughter!

When Mother won a brand new television in a supermarket sweepstakes drawing, she didn't put it in her bedroom. Instead she boxed it up and sent it to my sister and her family, who had never owned a television. And of course Dad supported her, as he does in all of her caring. Nor is he lacking in his own great love.

When he won some money in a drawing, Dad invested it immediately and then used both it and the profits to pay for each member of the family and their own individual families to fly to their home for a huge family reunion. How easy it would have been for him to buy a new car or boat with that money.

I am not bragging about my parents' kindness

and generosity, nor am I trying to bring to the attention of others their great goodness and righteousness. I am merely illustrating the love that has had such a profound effect upon my life. Now as I interact with my own husband and my own children, I am constantly remembering the loving acts of my parents. As I do, I find myself using their example in a very natural way in my own home.

Do we need to add to this? We doubt it, for the point is obvious. Consider now another sort of evidence of Deutch's Law as it relates to discipleship.

For nineteen years I've lived so close to a woman who is caring and giving, and I didn't even notice. She has always been there when I needed her, but I didn't realize it. She has taught me the best and most important knowledge on earth, the gospel of Jesus Christ. She has taught me how to get along with people, how to not quit, how to sort clothes, how to sew, and how to love. Still, I did not notice. Why? She was quiet when it became her turn to talk about her talents, so I thought she didn't have any. She always ran looking for my dad's socks, while I know that I would have told him to go find his own. She never bought lots of new clothes, so I thought she liked being out of style. She could never hold in her emotions, so I thought she was weak. Through my life I thought very little of her, while all the time she thought everything of me. Her never-ending quiet influence and example of caring have finally penetrated my thick skull, and at last I see that following her example is the way to becoming Christ-like. It has taken me all these years to understand that my mother's love is so quiet, yet so strong, that through all eternity I will be a product of it. Thank you, Mother!

5

Deutch's Law—love begets love. It is incredible how powerful this truth really is. Another of our friends wrote this:

> I have a sister who is two years older than I. When we were young, I thought Kris was the most beautiful, outgoing, wonderful person a girl could ever want for a sister. She was born with a cleft palate, and she has a slight, hardly noticeable scar on her radiant face. I always thought that everyone loved her, and I never knew that she had faced ridicule because of such a thing. I didn't notice the scar, and I couldn't imagine that anyone else did either. In fact, I was in my teens when Mother finally told me this story.
>
> One Sunday when Kris was a little girl, she was sitting around dejectedly watching everyone else dress for church. Mother noticed that she was not getting ready, sensed that something was wrong, and asked her about it. Kris answered matter-of-factly, "I'm not going to church. I don't believe in God anymore."
>
> When Mother asked her why, Kris began to cry, and finally she told of a boy at school who teased her every day about her scar. He taunted her and said cruel things about how ugly she looked.
>
> Kris had knelt by her bedside every night for months, asking God to make the boy stop saying cruel things to her. She had always been taught that God answers prayers, but because he didn't seem to be answering hers, she had decided that he must not really be there!
>
> Mother comforted Kris, found out who the boy was, and bore her testimony that the Lord was indeed there but usually answered prayers through his children on earth. Then she promised Kris that her prayers were indeed being answered. Then she told my father what had happened.

Heartsick, Dad telephoned the offending boy's father and in a very loving way told him of the situation. From that day on the problem was solved, and our entire family learned that God loves us and extends that love through our earthly parents— those who are his servants and partners in the rearing of his children.

Ideally, then, and this is according to God's plan, each of us should have been born into a loving family where two parents work in harmony with each other and with God to teach us that we are important and are loved. In such an atmosphere, we would easily learn to love others, and that is the most vital element in our ultimately becoming disciples of the Lord Jesus Christ.

This doctrine is supported by a plethora of scriptural evidence. One illustration is in Mosiah 4:14-15, where King Benjamin states: "Ye will not suffer your children that they go hungry, or naked; neither will ye suffer that they transgress the laws of God, and fight and quarrel one with another, and serve the devil, who is the master of sin, . . . he being an enemy to all righteousness. But ye will teach them to walk in the ways of truth and soberness; ye will teach them to love one another, and to serve one another."

An additional scripture to consider is found in the Doctrine and Covenants. In this passage the Lord says: "I have commanded you to bring up your children in light and truth. But verily I say unto you, my servant [put your name here, please], you have continued under this condemnation; you have not taught your children light and truth, according to the commandments; and [so] that wicked one hath power, as yet, over you, and this is the cause of your affliction." (D&C 93:40-42.)

Elsewhere the Lord defines light and truth as Christ and the Spirit of Christ, and of course Christ was the epitome of love, and his Spirit is the spirit of pure love. Translated then, the Lord seems to be saying that *if we as parents do not teach our children the pure love of Christ, Satan will have power over us and will be the cause of many afflictions to us.* Are you having afflictions in your life, and might that be the reason for them?

A corollary to the above thought might be that if we as grown children do not exhibit or manifest the love for each other that our parents diligently tried to teach us, then *we* might be the cause of much affliction in our parents' lives. Such a thought is truly frightening.

So in the proper and God-approved family situation, all children grow up in an atmosphere of love and kindness, and then they will rear their own children in the same manner. But this sort of atmosphere is the ideal; it is rarely what actually takes place. Often families are broken; just as often they are composed of one or both parents who do not know how to show love, or who do not understand the importance of doing so; and with frightening frequency there are no parents at all to give children that all-important start. Yet even under such difficult conditions, children show amazing resilience if given the chance, even by outsiders, to respond to love, as illustrated in the following story.

> As I entered the kitchen I noticed that I was late for family prayer. Again. But Dad said only: "Sit down. Your mother and I have a matter to discuss with the family."
>
> We then learned of a phone call from Brazil in which Dad had been told of a woman dying of cancer who had taken into her home twenty-four children who were under the age of three. Dad had been asked if our family would like to adopt twin boys from that group.
>
> We all reacted favorably to the idea, so on June 15 my parents flew to Brazil and checked into a hotel. Shortly thereafter a knock came on the door. Mother opened it, and there stood a man with two small boys. The boys were three years old but were

only twenty-seven inches tall (the size of a one-year-old). They were undernourished because they had lived on bread and coffee for their entire lives. They had big pot bellies and long blond hair, and the only clothes they owned were sacks that had been made into robes. They did not even own playthings, but they were delighted when they found some pieces of paper to play with.

These boys had many problems. They had been beaten each time they had forgotten to dump and wash out the cans they used for toilets. They had also been beaten if they forgot to roll up the paper they slept on. They were so used to these beatings that they would cry the instant that they sensed anger in anyone around them. So far as my parents could tell, the boys had never experienced an act of love from anyone, not even a smile.

My parents brought the children home and then took them to the UCLA Medical Center for testing. The research department diagnosed in both of them a maternal deprivation syndrome. This meant that their bodies were degenerating because of a lack of love. My parents were told that the boys had never experienced brain stimulation, and that their condition could eventually lead to a complete learning disability and finally to death.

The prognosis: no one knew. My parents were told that the only cure for maternal deprivation syndrome was intense care and love. Without it, the boys' life expectancy would be five to seven years.

Now, years later, our family takes pride in the fact that we have done our best for these brothers, making them as much a part of our family as any of the rest of us. Although our brothers still struggle with some things, they are growing and are now of average weight, and we are prayerfully hopeful for them in every aspect of their lives.

Amazing! Not only does the lack of love in a child's life set him up for years and perhaps eternities of misery, but it can also be physically deadly. And yet just simple caring, simple discipleship, can forever reverse that tragic process. Here are other examples of such love and caring, though from slightly different perspectives.

I was just four and a half years old when my parents separated and filed for divorce. Being so young but so teachable, I needed two loving parents and my brothers and sister in order to lay a strong foundation for my character. But this did not happen, for during the next year I was separated from all of my family except my brother Chris, who was two years older than me. For a year we were passed around between family and friends, and then the court system stepped in and we were placed in a juvenile home and held until our parents' divorce was final. Then we were to be placed for adoption.

But who would want two troublesome little brothers? We thought no one would. Even so, our silent prayers were answered when one day they walked into our lives: Aunt Pat and Uncle Sonny, as we called them. They cared enough to share with us their time, efforts, patience, and, most of all, love.

As I look back, I see what a sacrifice that must have been for them. My brother and I were pretty rough, and they understood that we would need even more of their time than their own sons. Yet still they took us in, and I am so thankful for that caring.

More importantly, I am thankful that our new parents loved the Savior and our Heavenly Father. They were Catholic, and they taught us so much in that faith. I owe them so much because of that. They taught me true and basic principles of Christianity, they showed true charity, and I am a member of The Church of Jesus Christ of Latter-day Saints today because of their faithfulness in living and teaching love in their home.

Oh, how much do I owe this family? All that I am today! They cared enough to give all they had to make me who I am. I know of two young men today that care more about others and themselves because someone they had never seen before said, "Yes, we will care enough to share until your own family cares enough to want."

Isn't it interesting to consider how far these ripples of caring might actually go, given the duration of eternity? And how many of God's children might be affected? Think of the value of the ramifications of such caring, especially when it is considered that the Lord exclaims concerning only one: "If it so be that you should labor all your days . . . and bring, save it be one soul unto me, how great shall be your joy with him in the kingdom of my Father!" (D&C 18:15.)

Nor should we think that true caring can be limited only to those who have a full understanding of Christ's gospel, as illustrated in the following quotation.

Even though she is not a member of the Church, my mother reminds me of President Spencer W. Kimball. Her motto seems to be "Do it," and then "Do it just a little bit more." It is amazing to study the things she does for our family. Our home is always immaculate, especially for when my father comes home. I did not appreciate the effort that required until Mother accepted a full-time summer job and her home responsibilities fell upon my shoulders. Up to that time, I had been quite spoiled. I rarely had to help with the dishes or do household cleaning, and all I was ever responsible for was my own room. Now I had to do the whole home, plus the cooking and so on, and still find time for a little fun (of course I couldn't give up my fun!). I soon found out that if I kept up her pace, I was exhausted and cranky by early afternoon. Mother always made sure that each of us had an ample supply of washed and ironed clothes to choose from. After I had assumed her role, the closets quickly looked bare. Anyone who "didn't have time" to make his bed had it made by my mother. Not anymore. There was just too much to be done.

By the end of the first week I noticed a change in the house. Despite my best efforts, all the little things weren't getting done. Nobody seemed to notice all that I did do, only those tasks that I missed, and did they ever complain! So Mother began doing overhauls of the house each weekend, trying to help me keep up.

Now, years later, I have come to appreciate that it is not the big things in life that are difficult to accomplish, but the myriad of little ones. Mother does all those little things and more, because she cares. It is easy to say that one cares but quite another to prove it through one's actions. My mother has set a grand example for me to follow, and it is my constant prayer to be like her—to care enough to do.

Ripples of caring—Deutch's Law exemplified. It is a constant marvel how simple a task it is to turn the heart of another toward good. Do good, and it will invariably happen. Nor does it need to be limited to family activity and caring only. Consider the following two experiences, and you will see what we mean.

When I look back and evaluate my life, I can see that I never would have made it without the special teachers and leaders I had in the Church. Once when I was quite small, I went to class early, and my Sunday School teacher asked me to straighten the chairs. Afterward she told me how much she appreciated my help, and from then on she didn't have to ask me to help again. I made a special effort to be early each week, and she always thanked me warmly for my assistance. I see now I was responding naturally to the caring of a true disciple of our Savior.

In high school I could have gone astray quite easily because of the friends I had chosen. The person who helped me most during that difficult time was another Sunday School teacher. He went out of his way not only to give interesting lessons, but to be a friend outside of class. He would always come up whenever he saw me to ask how I was doing, ask about school, and ask about my friends. Even though I acted embarrassed whenever he did that, he ignored my rudeness and was always friendly, and deep down I knew he cared and loved me. Today he is still one of my closest and most valued friends.

Ever since he had been a young boy, my brother Steve had owned a gentle old Hereford cow he called Nellie. The cow was his pet and was loved by our entire family.

One summer morning when Steve was thirteen, we went out to the pasture and found Nellie lying on her side. Her stomach was bloated, and she was thrashing around and kicking her feet, trying to get up. She could hardly breathe, and we thought she would die at any minute. Not knowing what else to do, we knelt down and offered a prayer. As we stood up, Nellie settled down and seemed to fall asleep. We ran up the hill and told Mother about the desperate situation, and the family decided to have a special fast that day for Nellie.

When Dad arrived home, we asked him if he would give the cow a blessing, because we loved her and thought sure that would help her. Dad agreed, and our family gathered around as Dad anointed her and blessed her. I think he must have felt a little funny doing that, but realizing that Nellie was God's creation too, and thinking of how much Steve loved his cow, Dad didn't hesitate to use his priesthood at all.

By that evening many of the men in the neighborhood had heard about the situation with Steve's cow, and they came over because they cared about Steve and wanted to help. At eleven o'clock that night there were ten concerned men in our pasture. Steve told them that he had learned from the vet that if Nellie did not get up soon, her legs would go bad. So, even if she recovered from the bloating, she would not be able to get up. The veterinarian had said it was possible to raise a cow up and suspend it in the air for short periods of time, thereby preventing its leg muscles from being adversely effected.

Willingly these good neighbors set out to lift Steve's two-thousand-pound sick cow into the air. They attached the pair of "hip-lifters" under the cow's hip bones, rigged up a pulley, and pulled on the rope. Our eighty-five-year-old home teacher was straining on the rope alongside our elders quorum president, an inactive neighbor, several other old farmers, and other concerned men in our community. Late into the night they worked, and I was so impressed at the concern they showed for Steve. You see, it wasn't the cow so much as it was my brother that they loved and cared about.

Now Steve is that way. No matter who needs help, he is always one of the first ones there to lend a hand.

As we look back through these experiences, we see a great deal of pain and suffering. Yet those factors do not

14

seem to matter if mixed with that suffering there have been love and concern. When these are present, the individuals involved have learned to give love themselves and thus have come to know the genuine happiness of discipleship. Even though that is desired, if such love is not present, at least in sufficient quantity to be noticed, then unhappiness will surely follow.

To illustrate, we would like to show you the other side of Deutch's Law. That is, *the less we act in loving ways, the more others around us respond in like manner.* In Dad's words, the ripples we send out are negative. Anger begets anger, cruelty begets cruelty, aloofness begets aloofness, cursing begets cursing, and on and on.

And as Dad explained that day in Sanpete County, those who treat others with cruelty or unkindness are in a precarious position. Even though they think it is only themselves who will suffer from their negative behavior, that is not true. They are actually sending out ripples, sowing seeds of selfishness in the minds and hearts of everyone around them, and they will ultimately be held accountable for the damage and possible destruction of those other souls. Said poetically by one of our friends:

> A child becomes what he thinks he is,
> Either a great big dummy or a great big whiz.
> What potential in him that will be found
> May be up to the people that he's around.

Consider the following incidents illustrating the negative side of Deutch's Law.

It seems that some people have to step on other people's heads so that they can feel a little superior. The problem this creates is that while people stomp all over everybody else's ego, they are also demeaning themselves, and soon no one remembers

15

that they are all God's children. I know. When I was young, I was one of those who was stomped on.

Day after day the kids at school made fun of me, and most of the time it reduced me to tears. I could never kick the ball straight in kickball or read the fastest or write well enough to be chosen to learn cursive or called up to talk about a movie I had seen. I felt like I was at the bottom of an endless pit.

Now I actually was not as bad as I thought, even though I made mistakes that no one forgot and did things right that no one remembered. But I did not think of myself as a child of God. Instead I got caught in the same trap as my classmates; I felt that if I was going to look good, I had to put somebody down first. My poor little brother ended up as that somebody, and that made two of us who were suffering.

And it didn't stop there. My younger brother became a monster to all the neighborhood pets. Our cat really had it bad, and every time my little brother was around, it would hide under the bed. That is how the cycle of not caring works. Even now, I have to continually remind myself that I am a child of God, and that I am okay.

Too many times we think that we are on a ladder where we need to step on others' heads before we can climb to the top. Actually, life is like a large staircase, and each step is big enough for any number of people. Wouldn't it be nice if everyone at least helped one person on the step below up to the next? Wouldn't it be nice if everyone thought, "I am a child of God, and so are you."

The person who wrote that feels miserable, and it is easy to see. Who do you suppose will be held accountable for that misery? And who do you suppose failed to be a barrier to the Satanically desired misery this person is suffering, or, in other words, failed to be a disciple of Jesus Christ? Rather frightening questions, aren't they? Now consider the words of another deeply hurt person.

> I fall under the classification of a loner. Sometimes I feel bad about it, but usually I don't. Still, it hurts when I see couples or groups talking and enjoying themselves because I have never had that happen to me. I think this is because I have no family ties—maybe a frayed string here and there, but nothing sturdy. I am the middle child of five, and we have never been close. I have no love for my father, and although I love my mother, it isn't a binding love. In fact, my younger sister and I have a running gag in which we pretend that our bedrooms are actually apartments in a complex. We talk as if we hardly know each other and complain about our crazy landlords (our parents). It's all a joke, but it is a true reflection of reality.
>
> At school I had occasional friends, but at home I had no one. My mother used to console me by saying that friends would come, but each time I have started to get a friend, that person ended up stabbing me in the back. Now I am very cautious about who I talk to. I don't allow myself to get attached to anyone, and I hide myself from almost everybody.
>
> I've thought about suicide several times, and a few times I've even planned how and when I'd do it. If I didn't know there was something more to this life than just existing here, I wouldn't be alive. In the 46th section of the Doctrine and Covenants, the Lord explains that to some it is given to "know." Well, I *know*. I think Heavenly Father blessed me with this gift, my testimony, so I wouldn't give up. That knowledge must have come from him, for it certainly didn't come from my home.

Again, where will at least some of the accountability for this person's misery rest? And how many people do you suppose have lost forever the opportunity to deflect pain and bring joy into this person's life?

The negative side of Deutch's Law was brought closer to home by an experience one of us had a few years ago with one of our sons (Brenton has seven sons and Blaine has four, and so we will do a bit of literary acrobatics in this account to camouflage the events so as to protect the guilty, meaning one of us).

Some time ago, when our family was somewhat smaller, I had great difficulty relating to one of my sons. I believe that we bring much of our personality with us from the pre-earth life, and so I barely tolerated this son's behavior. I excused myself as I spanked him daily, feeling somehow that his spirit was contrary and must always have been so.

As time passed, and I guess it was when this son was about five or six years old, I learned about Deutch's Law, and for the first time I allowed the Holy Ghost to impress upon my spirit the feeling that perhaps I was using my belief in premortal personality development to excuse the unloving and harsh way in which I responded to his misbehavior. He was always treating his brothers and sisters unkindly and seemed to delight in mistreating his mother. In short, in my eyes this son could do no good.

When I finally climbed down from my horse of defensiveness about this son's behavior, I considered for the first time that it might have been his father who was acting inappropriately and so I decided to conduct an experiment. I determined, even though I did not feel that I loved that son or even that I liked him, that I would tell him that I loved him several times a day and that I would begin hugging and kissing him just as often as I did the other children.

I am very serious when I say that it took this son

almost another five years of receiving loving and
caring words and deeds from his father before he
could (without prodding) tell me that he loved me.
At age eleven, he began to smother me with kisses,
and it has been some time since he has not at least
kissed me goodnight. And he is a *teenager!*

The intriguing part of this experiment (which,
by the way, was one of the most difficult patterns of
unnatural behavior that I have ever forced myself to
perform) is that gradually over time we have seen
this son's grades improve to where he is always on
the honor roll, he is a leader in his scouting and
priesthood groups, and his friends are drawn to him
like bees to honey. He has *become* a loving, caring
young man, simply because his parents (especially
his father) repented and treated him that way.

Perhaps one way to capsulize that account is to state that
we either live *up to* or *down to* our understanding of how
others around us expect us to live. It gives this father chills
as he thinks of how he nearly destroyed his relationship with
his son!

Now, as a conclusion to this chapter, consider the traits
of a true teacher of love.

As he thrust his cleaning rod down the barrel of his
gun, Wulf Wulfenstein forced the unnoticed shell
against the firing pin, and the gun discharged. The
blast caught him directly in the chest, dropping him
in a lifeless heap on the floor. It was February 12,
1974. Wulf Wolfenstein was dead.

We were playing in a deacons basketball
tournament, and our team was in top form, having
posted several victories that morning. Initially we
shrugged off the bad news, imagining that rumors
were being spread to break our concentration. After
all, only boys like ourselves had told us.
Nevertheless, each of us was beginning to consider

the possibility that the news was valid. When the incident was finally confirmed, a dull pain formed in my stomach, and I thought, "That's impossible! That could not happen to my scoutmaster."

My disbelief turned first to anger and then to sorrowful acceptance, and the other boys and I scanned in our memories times that had come about simply because of Wulf Wulfenstein.

He had been a bear of a man, 6'3" and 220 pounds. On our backpack trips, his pack had consistently weighed 75 to 80 pounds, and much of what he carried was ours. He played hard, he worked hard, and he had continually stated that he was just an overgrown boy.

Whatever he was, Wulf had been just what we had needed. He had been rough, and yet in his soft-spoken manner he had displayed a genuine concern and gentleness for each of us. When I moved into the ward, Wulf made a conscious effort to ensure my acceptance and progress on the ladder towards Eagle. He involved me right from the start, as he strove to make his troop a working unit. He gave us his time, interest, and continual attention. He obtained work projects from his company so that each of us could learn the value of hard work. Yet he was one of us in our playing, too. At summer camp he led our tent-dumping raids on other troop campsites. Snow would fly as he executed donuts on the ice or attacked snowdrifts with a van full of laughing Scouts. Yet his actions did not inspire rowdiness, but greatness. Every one of his Scouts obtained the rank of Eagle. They were not forced or pushed in their progress; Wulf simply inspired motivation. He always made progress seem important. He was willing to conduct his interviews with the boys at any hour of the day or night. Realizing that some Scouts tend to procrastinate, he accepted merit-badge cards up to one hour before a court of honor, and then he would rush out to pick up those extra badges. Wulf ensured that every moment of a Scout's progress was highlighted with care and shared with others. He pulled the entire ward to the court of honor ceremonies, attempting to stimulate increased ward interest in the boys he loved.

Wulf's sacrifice of his own time was unbelievable. Sometimes I wondered if his wife ever saw him, for he was endlessly with the Scouts. But with that kind of effort, our troop gradually improved. Soon we were winning all sorts of troop awards, and no matter where we went, there was not a troop like ours. Every Scout became an achiever, some more from pure admiration for Wulf than from anything else. The tie between him and us grew incredibly strong, for we knew that he cared about us and actually enjoyed spending his time with us. That is what made all the difference; that is what made Wulf great.

Then he died, and I thought the entire program would die with him. However, our parents had caught his spirit, and at his funeral I could see the quiet resolve forming among each of us, as well as our parents, to never let his caring ways stop. Our stake created a Wulf Wulfenstein Memorial Trophy to be used as a traveling award for the courts of honor, and still in our troop nearly every boy reaches the rank of Eagle. Wulf's practices and spirit have not been abandoned, and that is the ultimate tribute a group of people can pay to such a loving and caring man.

Each of us has many kinds of experiences. They may be filled with joy, sorrow, ecstasy, or pain. Eternally, those factors don't seem to matter much as long as someone is there to teach us love. If that occurs, we can then learn to have true charity, which is, of course, the essence of discipleship.

CHAPTER 2

DESTRUCTION AND DISCOVERY

I was in the seventh grade when I was told by an orthopedic surgeon that in order to save my right leg and be able to use it for the rest of my life, I would have to wear a full-length steel brace on it for approximately three years. Of course I was devastated because I knew I was going to be rejected and ridiculed by the kids I had tried so hard to be friends with.

The day quickly arrived when I went to school for the first time wearing the brace. When I walked into the building clanking along with the brace and the elevated shoe I wore on my other foot to make things come out even, I was about ten minutes late. As I maneuvered toward my locker, I overheard my "good friend" say to another of my "good friends" that there was no way she was going to be seen with a clomping, clanking freak like me. Besides that, she said, I probably had fleas anyway. I nearly cried, but I held my feelings in and hobbled silently to science class.

The class was taking a test, and although I was only a small catastrophe inching my way between the narrow-spaced seats, everyone still looked up disapprovingly. I could have died when I saw the horror and disgust on their faces and heard their surprised gasps and pitying moans. Again I nearly cried, but I held in my tears and pretended to take my exam.

At lunch I was horrified to discover that I did not have the capacity to navigate stairs. Consequently I could not get up to the building where lunch was served. I didn't dare ask anyone to bring anything down to me, for fear of how they would react. So I went into the dark English room and waited out the lunch hour. Again I felt like crying, and perhaps I lost a tear or two. But mostly I held my emotions in check, determined to be bigger than my trial.

After what seemed an eternity, school ended for the day. Since it was impossible for me to walk very far, my mother had to come and take me home. I chose to wait for her in the shelter of the principal's office, where I hoped that mean and rude comments wouldn't be uttered.

When Mother finally arrived, I tried to smile and look better than I felt.

"How did your day go?" my mother asked.

"Fine."

"Any trouble?"

"No."

"I'm proud of you, did you know that?"

I looked up at my mother and saw that she meant it, and finally, I cried.

A frequently asked and not so easily answered question is: How can children be so cruel to each other? Also, consider the even larger issue of cruelty between people of all ages. Why we damage each other's self-esteem becomes a very significant question.

Before we proceed further, we would like to clarify a common misunderstanding. Most people use the terms *self-concept* and *self-esteem* interchangeably. That is not correct, as each is vastly different from the other.

Self-concept is defined as *who or what we think we are.* In contrast, *self-esteem* is defined as *how we feel* about who we are. Usually people with positive self-concepts will also *feel* good about themselves and thus have a good amount of self-esteem. However, that is not always the case. For there are people who have a positive self-concept (even though it may be unjustifiably inflated) who deep inside themselves feel like complete failures. The damage we are discussing in this book relates to our self-esteem—how we *feel* about who we are.

Several years ago, during the filming of *Windwalker*, Blaine sat on a snowbank in the Uinta Mountains and listened as one of the actors, a fine man named Harold Gos Coyote, spoke of the ancient Native American tradition of the Pale God. Gus explained that this great being (whom the Book of Mormon identifies as Jesus Christ) told the people that competition was the ugly sister of opposition; that God had given mankind opposition to teach them strength; and that the evil one or Satan had then introduced competition as a counterfeit, set up to produce weakness and destruction among the people.

Father Lehi said it this way: "It must needs be, that there is an opposition in all things." (2 Nephi 2:11.) Alma expounds upon the principle of opposition in Alma 42. But nowhere, in all the scriptures, do we read of the glory and benefits of competition. It is not there, simply because it is not a principle of God.

Harold Gos Coyote went on to explain that the difference between competition and opposition was a matter of attitude. Given opposition, a man or a woman, in order to survive and to grow, must become better than their past selves. That is difficult, of course, but by no means impossible. On the other hand, if competition rules people's lives, then they spend their energies trying to become better than other people, a virtual impossibility according to God's laws. When such people ultimately realize that their task is unattainable and that they can *never* be better than all other people in all things, bitterness sets in, or remorse, or the loss of self-esteem, or any number of other ailments, and all are destructive to the God-like qualities of love for self and others that we have been sent here to mortality to develop.

"For instance," Harold asked Blaine, "who is your favorite writer?"

"Oh, probably Robert Ludlum or Louis L'Amour."

"Okay, I like Louis L'Amour too, so let's say it is him. Blaine, if Louis L'Amour is your competition, you and your brother Brent can never completely succeed as writers until he fails. Each flaw in his work is a cause of rejoicing for you, and each step he might take backward becomes a triumph for you as you feel that you have stepped forward.

"On the other hand, if Mr. L'Amour is your opposition, each success he achieves is also a triumph for you; you rejoice in each step he takes forward, and you ache when perchance he falls backward."

"Why?" Blaine asked quickly.

"Because the better he does, the better you must also do to keep him in sight. He has become your strength-producing opposition. You actually begin to rejoice in the successes of another.

"Now you claim that the Pale God is Jesus Christ, and so far as I know, the doctrine Jesus taught was love. Can you be a Christian if you do otherwise than love? Can you be a Christian if you are actually hoping for Mr. L'Amour's downfall? Of course you can't. That isn't love. The very idea is ludicrous!"

Up to that point a highly competitive person, Blaine began to consider for the first time the effects of competition upon his life and upon the lives of those around him—not the strivings to do better himself, but the strivings to do and be better than others.

And so we ask, after years of considering this ourselves, is competition inherently evil? Does it in fact create problems that make love between people vastly more difficult than would otherwise be the case? Does it frequently create problems that make love almost impossible?

One semester when we were teaching at Brigham Young University, we conducted a survey among our students and learned that they felt that sins today could be divided into four basic categories. They then revealed (from their perspective) the most difficult problems young men and young women had to overcome.

Clearly 92 percent of the boys felt that their greatest problem was lustful thinking and its consequences. This is truly a serious problem, and there may be no sin that is more insidiously destroying the effectiveness of God's Latter-day priesthood army. Immorality is rampant, and gross perversions of all that is sacred and holy fill the television channels, seep out of radio speakers, leer at us from the photographs of magazines, and crawl into our minds through the explicit writing contained in so many "legitimate" books.

Truly, in this war to thwart the plan of God and prevent the Second Coming of our Savior, Satan has attacked these warriors of God who are called his priesthood.

And why has he chosen this method? Because he is not stupid. He knows more clearly than we can imagine the literalness of the results of lustful thinking and immoral behavior. Listen to the words of the Lord: "He that looketh upon a woman to lust after her shall deny the faith, and shall not have the Spirit; and if he repents not he shall be cast out." (D&C 42:23.)

Think of that. Lustful thinking constitutes a denial of what we believe, and it makes it impossible for us to have the Spirit of the Lord. Can men exercise priesthood power, can they lead others, can they help bring about the second coming of the Lord Jesus Christ if they are denying his faith and have not his Spirit? Of course they can't, and of every being upon this earth, Satan knows that best of all. Consider, for instance, how the great King David was so effectively destroyed by the wiles of the Satanically inspired Bathsheba. (2 Samuel 11, 12; D&C 132:39.) Would that this tragic experience with lust and immorality could become a beacon of warning to *all* of God's priesthood holders. It does, and until we learn to plead for and exercise control over our minds and bodies, there will be great suffering and limited effectiveness within the Lord's earthly kingdom.

26

But in our BYU survey, surprisingly only 30 percent of the young women understood that so many of the young men struggled to such an extent with lustful thoughts about them and their eternal sisters. *They* thought that the boys' biggest problem was cruelty and unkindness.

What an unspoken sermon there must be in that assumption, which had to be based upon the way boys had treated them throughout their lives. To illustrate that, may we share an experience that occurred in one of our high-school classrooms just when we began teaching at BYU. It was the last week of the school year. One of us was teaching seniors, and one of those—a girl—came to our office, despondent. We'll relate this experience in first person, so you can feel the impact of the moment as it unfolded.

"How can I help you, Sis?" I asked, realizing that something serious was taking place in this student's mind.

"You probably can't," she responded, breaking into tears. "I just need to tell someone."

"Tell someone what?" I queried.

"What happened last night at the senior banquet," she murmured.

"Go ahead."

"Well, the class president got up and announced last night that, unbeknownst to the girls in the class, the senior boys have created a list over the past three years—a list in a black book that is passed around. In that book each of the girls in the senior class is rated from 'dynamite' to 'dog.' I'm one of the dogs."

Well, as one can imagine, I found it difficult to believe what she was telling me, but I continued to question her.

"What do you mean? How do you know how you have been rated?"

"Oh, it's easy. Last night the class president made the list public. *Everybody* knows now."

I was stunned! This young lady had not been on one date in her high-school career, and now she knew why. Only the girls who rated above a certain level were asked out. All others were considered unworthy of a date. I could hardly fathom how young men could be so cruel to the young ladies who where their peers. No wonder, as we learned at BYU, the girls felt so put down.

But girls have their own problems too. In the BYU survey we conducted 96 percent of the girls reported that their greatest trial was jealousy and envy, and almost 90 percent of the boys agreed.

As teachers, we questioned why there should be such apparently universal feelings of jealousy and envy among those young sisters, and finally from a young woman an answer came forward, as honest and classical an answer as any we ever received. "Brother Yorgason," she stated, "in our society, girls are products and boys are consumers. The market is highly competitive, and we girls have to be worried about packaging."

Did you catch that? The sense of competition helps to create these terribly inappropriate feelings of the need to always be better than someone else, and hence the ability to love is decreased.

Several years ago, Blaine had an experience with his wife, Kathy, that showed him that these feelings, manifested by jealousy and envy in younger girls, do not simply go away as girls mature. Instead, the feelings change and become inner rather than outward directed. Mature women who have struggled with self-esteem problems when younger now feel inadequate, unable to cope, and terribly unworthy of God's attention and blessings. In the following account, Blaine describes his wife's struggle with this problem.

It was late, and I was home alone, waiting for Kathy to return from Relief Society. I heard the car enter the garage and the door close, but then I heard nothing further from Kathy.

Becoming concerned, I got up and walked through the house. Nothing. Now worried, I looked more closely, and finally I found my sweetheart sitting at the back of our bedroom closet, weeping.

"What's wrong?" I asked.

"N-nothing."

Now I had lived long, and so I had developed tremendous insight into the heart of my beautiful wife. Therefore, with all of that insight, I knew that she was fibbing! So with great compassion and much coaxing, I dragged her out of the closet and into my studio.

"Okay," I asked pleasantly, "what seems to be the problem?"

"Nothing. Except that I . . . I'm *never* going to Relief Society again!"

"You what?"

"I mean it! I'm never going back!"

The silence that followed seemed to last forever. "But why?" I finally questioned, shocked at this great sign of apostasy.

"Because I'm not as good as those other women!"

"But—but of course you are!" I ordered her to believe.

"I am not! And furthermore, I'm not a good member of the Church, and I'm never going to make it to the celestial kingdom!"

Well, that *really* shocked me. After all, that was why I had married her in the first place (besides the fact that she was cute). I fully intended her to drag me along as she climbed upward. I mean, without her I didn't have a chance at all.

"Sure you are," I said, desperately trying to soothe her. We talked then, or rather I talked, and finally out came the reason why she didn't think she would ever make it.

My dear wife didn't feel like she could quilt or do those other handicrafty things!

"Horrors," I declared. "Oh no, oh no, oh no!"

Kathy pulled a face at me, and so I got serious. "Kath, there isn't a scripture *anywhere* that says you have to quilt or own a glue gun to get into the celestial kingdom."

"Oh no?" she asked. "I'll tell you what. You put on a skirt and go to Relief Society, and you'll soon find out differently!"

"I can't," I grinned.

"Why not?"

"They wouldn't let me in. My legs are too hairy, and besides, you don't have a maternity skirt anyway."

"Maternity?"

"Yeah. That's the only size that would fit me."

Kathy threw her shoe at me then, and once more she grew serious.

"Quilting and handicrafts aren't all," she stated hollowly. "Have you taken time to notice the Anderson kids? They are always neat and clean, and their hair is always in place. On the other hand, have you noticed ours? Two minutes out of the tub and they look like they just cleaned out Grandpa's pig pen. And ———'s hair hasn't been combed for longer than thirty-five seconds since the day he was born!

"I'll tell you something else, too! When the Swensons eat they play classical music in the background and talk about edifying and intellectual things. Have you noticed the conversations at our meals? We have Tom T. Hall singing 'Sneaky Snake' in the background while at the table we are experiencing World War III, only with leftovers instead of C rations. I'm telling you, Blaine, I am a failure as a mother, a woman, and a wife! There is too much to do, and I can't do it, and so I am not going to make it!"

Finally comprehending my wife's deep feelings, I at once settled down. In the mission field, when we had a contact who just wouldn't commit to baptism, or who couldn't see a reason why he should, we always made two lists for him. One showed all the reasons why he *should* be baptized, and the other showed all the reasons why he *shouldn't.* Then we stacked the list where he should, and that person usually got baptized shortly thereafter.

"Kathy," I smiled, "let's make a couple of lists."

She reluctantly agreed, so we did. I made only one mistake: I let her start with all the things she felt she had to do but couldn't. Here is her list:

In order to get to the celestial kingdom, I must:
  Keep my home clean
  Make my home attractive, with the right kind of atmos-
    phere
  Prepare menus at least a week in advance
  Shop for the best bargains
  Keep within our budget
  Save money by making clothes for children, and then by
    making them over again for the smaller ones
  Have as many children as I can considering my health—
    if I have two I feel I should have eight; if I have eight
    I feel I should also be doing civic things
  Teach my children:
    The gospel
    To love each other
    To be honest
    To be obedient
    To be industrious
    To be talented
    To be clean
    To be healthy
    To be safe
    To be sensitive to nature
    To be creative
    To clean their teeth
    How to prepare talks
    How to do math and science
  Do things with the children
  Expose the children to cultural events (ballets, plays,
    concerts)
  Make sure the children learn to play a musical instrument
    and practice an hour a day

Form carpools for everything on the face of the earth
Deliver kids to every place on the face of the earth at least
twice daily
Get kids to school and Church meetings on time
Read to the children
Take time to listen to the children's stupid "guess whats"
Keep boys caught up with Cub Scouts and merit badges
Be a nurse when anyone in the family is sick, including
myself
Have attractive table settings
Understand nutrition and plan all meals accordingly
Plan stimulating conversations at meals (no more World
War III)
Learn to sew and quilt and do handiwork—ugh!
Bake my own bread—and grind wheat for it
Attend sacrament meeting and Primary with kids
Attend Relief Society (I can't because I am in Primary, so
I feel guilty!)
Do my visiting teaching and take special interest in sisters
Be aware of neighbors' needs—when sick take in meals,
etc.
Be a missionary to nonmember acquaintances
Carry out Church responsibility in Primary
Feel responsible for each child in class
Attend temple regularly
Do genealogical research
Write in journal daily
Write letters weekly or monthly to family, friends, shut-
ins, all missionaries in ward
Keep track of your (husband's) home teaching families'
birthdays
Buy milkshakes for all above birthdays
Stay healthy
Eat proper food
Get enough exercise—30 minutes of running, cycling,
etc.
Do 15 minutes of waist and tummy flatteners for you
(husband)
Have good personal hygiene—be clean
Be beautiful—make-up, hair, clothes that are the right
season-color for my complexion

Support my local:
  political party
  symphony guild
  PTA
  current Mother's March
Develop my talents—music, art, dance, tennis
Read good literature—and you (husband) say that in-
  cludes all your dumb books
Read the scriptures daily
Pray several times a day
Do two batches of wash a day and all the ironing
Get plenty of rest
And least but definitely not last, be at the door looking
  ravishing each evening when you (husband) get home!

I learned later that Kathy had obtained most of this list
from our friend Diane Pace, and though I thought of making
a list of my own, I didn't. I mean, all I could think of was: get
up, shave, shower, wait for shirt to be ironed, get dressed,
wait for shoes to be polished, wait for breakfast, and so on.

My dear wife was in a great deal of pain, and in the years
since I discovered that she was, Brent and I have learned
that such pain is not at all uncommon. Constantly (and for
some reason this seems especially true of the sisters), we
compare ourselves with each other. We see where others
have achieved and where we haven't, we see where something is going right for them that isn't for us, and we become
devastated.

Frankly, that must not happen. Most of us want to be
perfect; after all, we have been so commanded. What we
forget is that we are mortal, and that with such a limitation,
we are given a great portion of eternity to work on perfection. Improvement we can achieve. But perfection? Highly
unlikely, at least in mortality.

Now, some of us are good at quilting and handicrafting,
some at leadership, some at mothering, some at studying
and learning, some at teaching, and so on. The list is almost
endless.

But no one is good at them all, and a sense of competition to accomplish them all immediately, because we erroneously think another has, is wrong!

Kathy's list, therefore, should become a long-range set of goals, a list of things to work toward accomplishing throughout mortality, not just tomorrow. To feel that we must do everything immediately, because it looks like so-and-so is doing everything, is one of the great and evil products of unrighteous competition.

Nor is competition a problem only among women. *Something* caused the boys mentioned in our BYU survey to show cruelty and unkindness. Might it have been the same problem manifested slightly differently—the idea that pulling down some weaker person (a girl) would somehow make the boy look stronger?

Our society places tremendous value upon competitive success, especially for young men, and those who succeed are given rich rewards. But beyond the relatively few young men who do achieve, how do the countless other non-achievers compensate to salve their riddled self-esteem and to end the ridicule of their friends? Somehow they must find a way to look as tough, as virile, as "macho" as their peers. And the easiest way seems to be to find a victim, a weaker person to look tough against.

A young lady wrote this:

> How do you feel concern or have a liking for someone that you have actually hated since you were seven years old? I'm speaking of one of my brothers.
>
> I have had a *lot* of talks with my parents about my feelings for him, but they always told me that I didn't hate him, but only disliked him. I have never even told them why I hated him, for I didn't (and don't) want to hurt them.
>
> Nor will I say here why I hate him, nor why it started when I was seven years of age. I will only say that he caused me great pain, and he was so much

bigger and just wanted to feel tough and to look "macho" in front of his friends.

When I was twelve, for instance, I went to call my mother on the phone. As I was dialing, my brother yanked the phone out of my hand. As can be imagined, that started a fight. He kept throwing me against the wall until he knocked me unconscious. He became worried at that and was really sweet to me after I regained consciousness. However, that only lasted until I tried to call my mother again. The fighting resumed, and we somehow ended up in the kitchen. I grabbed a bunch of knives and told him to leave me alone. He got them away from me, and then his anger got the best of him and he stabbed me below the shoulder. I think he was more shocked than I was, but he certainly didn't learn much.

It seemed to me that after that day he was always using me as his punching bag. Time after time he hurt me both physically and mentally, and it always started because he had to look tough in front of his friends.

Somehow this boy received the message (from those he wanted for his friends) that he wouldn't be accepted unless he did certain things to prove his strength, courage, and prowess. Even though he was not in an athletic contest, he began competing for friendship in a physical and terribly immature way, and he nearly destroyed his sister in the process. Most certainly he destroyed her natural affection for him, and her own fragile self-esteem took as complete a beating as she did. How much damage he also did to himself we can only guess.

In the July 1983 *Field and Stream,* in an article entitled "Competition vs. Sport," George Reiger writes: "The lack of competition—which lies at the heart of bona fide sport—makes [it] seem dull to readers and . . . television viewers. The entire point of sport is that it is something you must do yourself [alone—not against a competitor] to have any value at all.

"Competition within yourself," he continues, "never ceases. You are always trying to do better . . . than you did previously."

The message is clear. To do better than someone else is not to do better at all. Nothing has been proven from such a contest, for no two people or groups can ever be equally matched. Yet continually we promote such contests, fostering the idea that some people can and should be better than others. Who knows of the damage that is done thereby?

The desert of southern California in the summer is the next place to hell. The heat is scorching, stinging, and dry, and there I grew up. Our games and activities during the day were in my friend Doug's pool. Late afternoon found us playing baseball in the cul-de-sac (intense, screaming debates between each play because it seemed so important that we each win over the others). At night we played flashlight tag games.

The "gang" consisted of my best friend, Doug; his brother Stan; a fat kid with glasses named Paul; a skinny kid called John; a girl named Lynn; Stan's friend Mike; a panel of dignified ambassadors from nearby streets; and me.

And then there was Jeff Hobbs—or Snobbs, Blobbs, Stupid, Geek, Jerk, Baby Jeff, and other harsher names. Jeff was despised by all, and we used him to prove our own strength and superiority to each other. He was always a little fatter, slower, and less "cool" than we were. He had a lisp and a funny voice, and when we belittled him, we somehow felt that we were making ourselves look a little better.

Jeff was a pseudo member of the gang, but he was always the receiver of the hits, blows, curses, and criticisms that the rest of us might offer. Jeff was the scapegoat and the eighth-string right fielder who was only allowed to play when someone else couldn't be there. He was also allowed to swim with us, but only if we were playing Marco Polo "Stanley Style". That was a barbaric treatment of the original Marco Polo where those who were not "it" could hit, slap, kick, and tug at the person who had his eyes closed and was "it." Jeff was not a good swimmer and so was an easy target. I remember many times when he went running home in tears, often with a bloody nose or a cut. The door would slam and the curtain in his living room would part, and he would spend the rest of the day watching our activities while we laughed and made fun of him.

Jeff was tough, though, and he would usually return to our torture the next day, even though that torture seemed to be relentless and never-ending. Nor, so far as I can remember, did any of us ever change, and now I feel terrible about that.

As far as I know, Jeff graduated from high school, holds a job, lives with his parents, and has no really good friends. Nobody I know of really knows who Jeff is; he is just some stupid jerk left over from a diminishing childhood memory.

What is Jeff really like? I don't know either. I talked to my friend Doug about a month ago and asked him about Jeff. He said, "Oh, that geek? He's still around."

How tragic is this account! Considering the duration of eternity, how long will those negative ripples keep going out, and how far will they spread? Because we have all known a "Jeff," the question and the implications of its answer are terrifying.

In the July 1983 *Success* magazine, in an article by Robert Meier entitled "Are You Too Competitive?" we read the following:

Jealousy, competitiveness, and envy are emotions that eat away at us from the inside. All too often they spur us to behavior that is wasteful and ultimately self-destructive. . . . Some people object to the idea that competitiveness is an unhealthy drive. After all, they say, isn't it one of the primary motivations behind striving to get ahead and be successful?

The answer lies in the distinction between competing for a reasonable goal and competing for the goal of being "better." Self-esteem is at stake. [This is the reason competitiveness is closely related to jealousy and envy.] Striving to get ahead in order to obtain the benefits that come with [such advancement] is one thing; most people enjoy increased authority, pay and perks. But striving to get ahead *for its own sake,* in order to feel like a superior person, is unhealthy motivation.

Likewise, winning at games and contests is nice, to be sure. But *needing* to win . . . is also an undesirable motivation. So is the need to be smarter, better looking, wealthier, thinner, or more accomplished than others. All these needs reveal an underlying preoccupation with being a "superior person," as well as its flip side: the dread of being inferior.

One of our friends wrote this account.

When I was 10, my sister and I watched American Bandstand one Saturday, and I laughed at a fat girl dancing with a skinny guy. The next Monday our teacher tested our eyes and checked our height and weight. "Height: 5'1"," he called to the recorder. When he started moving the weight measure up the scale, nothing happened. He pushed it clear to the end—still nothing. Then he put the bottom weight at 100 pounds, and the top weight balanced at 20 pounds.

"One hundred twenty pounds," he called out to the recorder. The whole class stopped their schoolwork, and after a silent hush of disbelief, there was a collective gasp. So began the label of "Fatso" and a lifetime of battling weight.

Sixth and seventh grades I just endured—no one wanted a fatso at their parties, at movies, or to associate with. Finally I was diagnosed as having thyroid problems. I got some pills, and I began to lose weight. I was so happy because at last I was going to become "the same" as my friends. In fact, I helped the process along. I took too many pills, I bought chocolate laxatives and ate them like candy, and after every meal I forced myself to throw up. But I was losing weight, and I felt like I was as good as my friends, so I felt wonderful. During ninth grade I even danced with a couple of boys. By graduation, I looked beautiful, and I was accepted!

But then came summer and the fat, and by tenth grade I had a new nickname: the "Pink Elephant." The following three years brought skipped meals, fad diets, one blind date three days after my sixteenth birthday, and a self-esteem problem that I see now was even larger than I was. I was fat and ugly, and I knew it, and until I had somehow forced my body into the same shape and mold as those gorgeously thin bodies of my peers, who were always reminding me that I needed to do exactly that, I would never be any good for *anything!*

It is good and desirable to be healthy, of course, but our society's present preoccupation with the "body beautiful" leaves many among us, who are not so proportioned nor indeed can be, filled with pain and loneliness and great doubt about our own self-worth, simply because we do not look like everyone else. A competition factor? Yes. A creator of jealousy? Yes. Destructive of the ability to love self and therefore others? Of course!

The article "Are You Too Competitive?" continues:

Competitiveness and jealousy usually have their roots in childhood . . . [and may come from] sibling [or peer] rivalry or parental favoritism, [or a parental] message to the child that he is—or is supposed to be—better than, or even the best among, his classmates, his circle of friends, his cousins, or any comparison group. Or a child may develop these traits [simply] by identifying with a jealous and competitive parent.

Whatever the origin, these feelings may become established within the child's personality as habitual and preeminent emotions. Then most—if not all—personal encounters become competitive events . . . [upon] whose outcome the child bases his approval and liking for himself.

Jealous competitiveness, once rooted in the personality, tends to persist into adulthood, giving rise to oneupmanship and keeping up with the Joneses [or the converse lament "The grass is always greener on the other side of the fence"]. The competitive and envious person hates the neighbor with the [whatever] he himself can't afford, or else he exceeds his budget to buy [such things] for show. He frequently measures his career and monetary [and spiritual] accomplishments against those of his peers . . . and is enraged if his wife [or husband] pays [courteous] attention to other men [or women].

The psychological price of these traits is a big one. The competitive person often suffers self-doubt, feelings of helplessness, jealous rage and hurt, and the ache of envy.

With this idea in mind, read the pain and loneliness and longing to be accepted that come from between the lines of the following account, a vivid description of an inappropriate response to the need to feel accepted.

I have a roommate who ought to go in the *Guiness Book of World Records* because she has done almost everything there is to be done in this world that is unbelievable, incredible, or dangerous, and so she has firsthand experience in everything. What is so sad about this is that she actually believes these great lies. She not only fakes out a few gullible people, she actually fakes out herself.

She has had this terrible pain in her abdomen for the longest time, but she won't see a doctor. She would rather lie on the couch in the living room and let the agony on her face put all the rest of us through Pain 101 so we will try to comfort her. She also has this habit of fainting whenever a guy she likes is around. She doesn't mind it a bit when he puts his arms around her to pick her up. To her, that means he likes her. Of course, she hasn't been on a date in five years, and all she knows about romance is what she learns from her novels, but still she won't change. I have never known such a totally lonely person, and I wish I knew what had happened in her past that had caused her to behave in this manner. Then maybe she would let us become her real friends.

The *Success* magazine article concludes: "But the greatest damage done is the blocking of . . . self-development and the thwarting of genuine self-interest. Competitiveness is a consuming disease. It drains constructive and creative energies from their proper channels—personal fulfillment [and growth] in the social, recreational, family, and occupational spheres—and squanders them on a meaningless [and impossible] enterprise."

In other words, competitiveness against each other, which American Indian tradition tells us the Pale God taught so strongly against, is dangerously destructive to the capacity God placed in all of us to learn to love. Somehow competitive feelings, when directed toward other people, circumvent our natural inclinations toward kindness, and we become hardened not only toward each other but also toward ourselves. The Lord commanded: "Thou shalt love thy neighbor *as thyself.*" (Leviticus 19:18; italics added.) Interestingly, that very capacity to love, which Mormon called charity or the pure love of Christ, and which Jesus Christ himself exemplified perfectly, is what is required of us before we can become his true disciples.

Yet we continue, in so many ways, to foster the spirit of competitiveness among ourselves and our children. Winning

41

so frequently becomes more important than doing better as we pit our children against each other in scripture chases and pinewood derbies and baptism contests and athletic events; being the best becomes more important than being better as we compare ourselves with our associates while we vie for ecclesiastical or career positions or haul truckloads of materials to Relief Society to present our lessons because so-and-so did at least that much last week, and on and on and on.

One of us went to Florida on his mission. We won't tell you which one it was, but Blaine spent his mission in the Chicago area. Anyway, during a preparation day in Jacksonville, one of us was washing the missionary Plymouth with the assistant to the mission president. This missionary asked the assistant why he wasn't interested in baptism statistics.

This assistant, whose name was Mark Webb, stopped washing the car, smiled, and then shared his guideline to life. Simply stated, it is this: "There is no nobility in being superior to another person. True nobility is in being superior to one's past self."

Needless to say, this philosophy stuck with the other missionary we haven't named—and has likewise become his guideline to life.

Several years ago, during a time of personal struggle, Blaine recorded the following questions in his journal: "When will we learn that God's greatest act of creativity is our own individuality? When will we learn that we cannot truly love God until we have trusted His judgment implicitly, without arrogance and without complaint, as regards our own person?"

Let us repeat those questions. When, indeed, will we learn? Instead of showing and teaching gratitude to God for our own or our children's unique characteristics, most of us, even within the Church, forge ahead according to the competitive philosophy of the land, striving to be just a little better than everyone else. And thus we inadvertently teach our children that they must be even better than others just to be acceptable.

It is no wonder that cruelty and a lack of love abound in our society. Because of our competitive philosophy and its negative ramifications, unkindness to others, in one form or another, has almost become a necessity for our emotional survival. Cruelty has become a spiritually devastating plague upon the land. And thus the destruction of our esteem and capacity to love continues. Consider this:

A gust of wind pierced my body, mocking my windbreaker's feeble resistance. As it mercilessly knotted my hair and whipped it into my face, and laughed at my half-hearted attempts to untangle it, boiling clouds hovered menacingly. Suddenly a warm voice flavored with a Scottish brogue interrupted my silent battle with the wind.

"Why Nadine, I dinna know you war 'ome. How long 'ave you bin 'ere?"

"Two days, Mrs. MacIsaac," I responded, warmed by the unaffected concern so typical of these elderly people.

"And 'ow was BYU?" she asked.

I smiled at the incongruous mixture of BYU and a Cape Breton accent. "It was so exciting!" I replied. "I just loved it."

"Good. Are you 'ome fer the summer, dear?"

My smile faded, and my heart filled with the pain that thoughts of "home" always gave me. "No, I'm heading for Alberta right away."

"My goodness but yer a one fer travelin'. Yer never 'ome."

Pain flickered through me. "Itchy feet, I guess."

"Well, it was nice talking to you, dear. Tell yer mother I'll be droppin' by fer a pot o' tea one o' these days."

I smiled and waved, the wind's icy fingers probed my insides, and I shivered and walked away.

As I turned the corner, my elementary school came into view. The teeter-totter creaked and groaned while the swings swayed forlornly in the wind. As I stood there my mind went back, and my hands clenched—

Crack! My head snapped and I stumbled backward. Then my trembling hand found the scarlet imprint on my cheek as malicious eyes bored into mine.

"C'mon, hit me, you sniveling idiot! You think you're so hot just because you're new here!"

Crack! My eyes watered as her hand once again made contact with my face. The crowd of children snickered. "Hit her," my mind screamed frantically. But the message never reached my nerves. My hands remained motionless, and no words formed.

"Fraidy-cat! Fraidy-cat!"

I turned and headed for my home while hands pushed, feet kicked, mouths taunted, and I wept.

The wind whistled around my head, blowing strands of hair into my face. Absently brushing them aside I walked away from the school yard. The next bend in the road brought another brick building, larger and more complicated. Oh yes, how could I forget my fun-loving, flirtatious high-school days.

Someone snickered. Lunches were forgotten as kids eyed the entrance. With composure born of long and painful experience, I continued to walk.

"Is that a wiggle or a broken hip?"

The crowd sneered. I sat down and took out my lunch. Footsteps came closer, but I stared fixedly at my paper bag and did not look up. Elbows propped themselves negligently onto my desk and knees prodded me in the back. Whispering in stiletto voices dripping honey, they began to mock me:

"Hi, Nadine!"

"How are you, *Nadine?*"

"Lead bottom."

"*You* are just something else, aren't you, *Nadine.*"

The bell rang. Fingers tugged viciously at my hair.

"It was so-o-o nice talking to you, Nadine."

I sat stiffly, blindly, until the classroom was empty. Then, clutching my uneaten lunch, I walked into the hall. The silence was shattered as male voices began abusing me with their familiar taunts.

"Na-dog."

"Frog legs."

"What a wiggle."

"O-o-oh, how are you, Nadine?"

I continued to walk, retaliating, as always, with silence. Then I was kicked, and after all the years the last straw was broken. Eyes blazing, I whirled around and kicked the boy viciously in the stomach. His friends stared, frozen, as he fell back with eyes bulging. I lunged toward him, picked him up, and threw him hard to the cement floor. Then the mask of my eternal pain slipped back into place, I picked up my books, and walked away.

The wind still tore at me, and suddenly what was left of the bonds of family and friends disintegrated under the cold but searing memory of seven years of persecution. The haunting taunts tore at my mind, reopening old wounds that might never heal, and I knew that I could never come back.

"Na-dog!"

"Fraidy-cat!"

"Frog legs."

"Lead bottom."

Instantly I began to run . . .

Finally Main Street loomed, and with it the safety of my destination. Breathing hard, tormented, not knowing whether or not I would ever be worth anything but still anxious to try, I dashed into the office.

"I . . . I'd like to buy a plane ticket to Alberta, please."

Believe it or not, this is a true story. Unfortunately, such destruction of others is not limited to children and the ungodly. Even good and well-meaning people get caught up in the trap of pitting one human being against others, a trap that the Evil One has so cunningly set.

The summer I was thirteen, my mother (who is the religious backbone of our family) was away all summer renewing her teaching certificate. My brother had just returned from Viet Nam, and my father, to help my brother out emotionally, used almost every Sunday to take the rest of the family to see him. It was a three-hour drive each way, and it meant that we almost always missed our meetings.

Then one Sunday morning we didn't go to see my brother, so I went to church. In class our teacher started at one end of the room and went from child to child telling us our batting average, which he'd made up from our attendance. He came to my girlfriend who was sitting next to me and said, "You're batting 100 percent." Then he looked at me and said, "You're batting zero, and if you keep it up, you'll go to hell!"

I wanted to cry, it hurt so bad. I was like any other person, and I really cared what my friends thought. Now both they and I knew the truth: I wasn't a worthwhile human being. I walked out, not really knowing where I was going, but knowing for certain that I didn't have a chance with that man. From then on I skipped classes until he was released as our teacher.

Fortunately, years later, that teacher met the young girl, who by then had become a married woman, and apologized for what he had done to hurt her. Now both have sweet feelings toward each other. But not always do things turn out so positively.

One of our friends tells of a pretty cheerleader girlfriend of hers who got caught up in Satan's wiles, trying to be popular, and became known as the school drunkard and school tramp. She was involved with drugs; had moral problems; three times was taken by ambulance to the hospital, where she miraculously survived close brushes with death; and finally came to grips with herself and decided to repent and put her life in order.

She worked long and hard at upgrading herself, and the process, while agonizingly slow, nevertheless occurred, and her spirituality grew apace. Her grades improved; she radiated the light of the gospel; she was elected homecoming queen; she traveled to different wards to tell the young girls of her terrible experiences and the grief and hell that sin brings to a person. She did all in her power to repay the Lord for his merciful forgiveness.

Our friend concludes with this:

It is sad that the story can't end here. Julie left her past behind and eagerly came to BYU, where she found great happiness. She finally found what had always been missing when she had been younger: acceptance. Her friends loved her, and she continued to develop into a more pure and lovely young woman.

Sadly, she has just learned that people who knew her before, LDS people both at home and at school, returned missionaries, elders, future Relief Society presidents, and homemakers, are still talking about her, exaggerating her past into terrible accounts, persuading friends not to date her or associate with her, saying that she would only bring them down to her level.

They say, "A person like her can't change."

What a grievous sin these people are committing. Night after night I've watched Julie cry herself to sleep, and I've seen her self-respect, something that has taken her so long to rebuild, being slowly torn apart and shredded by these people. How sad this makes me feel, for her and for them as well!

Obviously the Lord cannot be happy when one of his children suffers such a deep loss of self-respect and self-love. In one way or another, therefore, whether in mortality or later, he will ultimately see to it that such a suffering child is made aware of his great love.

When Joseph Smith allowed Martin Harris to take the first 116 pages of the Book of Mormon manuscript and show it to Martin's restless wife, the Lord taught Joseph an interesting and pertinent lesson. When the manuscript was lost, Joseph was told not to retranslate that portion of the manuscript, because evil men had altered the words and would attempt to portray him as a fraud. Centuries earlier, however, the Lord had forseen such an attempt by Satan to destroy His work, and He had inspired Mormon to include two accounts of the same events—the book of Lehi (the lost manuscript), and the writings of Lehi's son Nephi. Joseph, therefore, was instructed to translate Nephi's work but to ignore the previously translated work of Lehi that covered the same historical events. To Joseph, the Lord said: "The devil has sought to lay a cunning plan, that he may destroy this work." (D&C 10:12.)

It appears to us that with the principle of competition, the devil is up to his old cunning tricks. His hope is to destroy God's plan by destroying God's children, by making them miserable like himself.

As with the Prophet Joseph, however, the Lord has prepared for Satan's destructive ploy. He has done so through the power of *love*. We have the opportunity, as mortals, to give love to others. But if we should not do so, then God most certainly shall. Consider the following illustration:

It was hard for me to really respect who I was. I felt that others were better than I was. My friends' families were all active in the Church, and mine wasn't. My parents didn't attend regularly, although they did encourage me to attend. This made me feel inferior to the other kids at church. Somehow I felt that the Lord loved them more than me because they had an active family.

Often I felt that the Lord had blessed others more than me. They had more talents that I had, and they were good in everything they did: sports, music, grades, and everything else. I always seemed mediocre, and I would think that there was no reason to even attempt to develop my talents, because I could never be as good as they were.

Finally I started asking the Lord why I had so many problems and why he loved others more than me. At that time the Spirit prompted me to get my patriarchal blessing. So I did, and what an experience!

In receiving it, I learned that the Lord loved me as much as anyone else, and that he had blessed me with everything I needed. I learned that he had sent me to my family for a purpose, and that now I must fulfill it. I also learned that I had been blessed with talents, and that I should develop them.

Through knowing that he really cared, I have been able to gain a great deal of confidence in myself. I am honored and proud to be a daughter of God, and slowly I am overcoming my fear of trying to be a better person.

Although the Lord lifts us, it also seems to us that one of the best ways for people to be lifted up after they have been knocked down is to have that lifting done by other people who have been moved by the Spirit of the Lord to do so. This accomplishes two things. First, it adds strength and goodness to the person doing the lifting. And second, it surely must restore a portion of a battered individual's faith in mankind, and thus in himself.

In conclusion, let us share the experience of one such boy who was very successful but who was not above "stooping" to help others.

Lee Bush was a young, slender, thirteen-year-old boy with horn-rimmed glasses, buckteeth, and cowlicks. He was also a victim of cerebral palsy. But even though his body was not well, his mind was. So Lee was a prisoner.

Day after day he would struggle to write his assignments, to speak clearly, and even to force his way down the school hallways. And every day, the same crowd of boys would harass Lee by shouting, "There goes the best-looking guy in the school!" or "Why don't you try out for the track team, Lee?" Also, they would continually steal his lunches or his meal ticket for hot lunch. Yet Lee seemed to take it all in stride, and he only looked sad as he went on his way.

One afternoon Lee endeavored to hobble over to the cafeteria, which was the farthest building on the campus from his special-education building. By looking at him, I could tell that he was having a particularly difficult time that day. Still, the usual crowd of boys surrounded him and began harassing him. Then they grabbed his sack lunch and began playing "keep-away" with it. As the sack bounced on the ground, the contents spilled out and were ruined.

Lee struggled to shout at them to stop, but he couldn't get the words out. Finally, after all the food was destroyed, they began to walk away. At that, Lee sat down and began to cry. The boys laughed, but I could tell that they felt uncomfortable.

Then suddenly Jim Chirgwin, the "jock" of the school, walked up, sat down next to Lee, and put his arm around his shaking shoulder. For a few minutes all he did was talk and comfort. Then he lifted Lee up, walked him to the lunch line, and bought him his meal. When they were through eating, Jim escorted Lee to his class. Lee tried to express his thanks, but he could only manage a crooked smile. Needless to say, no one picked on Lee anymore.

The trouble was, I was one of the "silent majority," the innocent bystanders who stood by and thought those boys were awful but who was just as guilty as they were because I did nothing to stop them or to help Lee. It took seeing what Jim did to make me realize that all of us have the responsibility to help *everyone* know that they are important, and that they are wanted and needed by all of the rest of us.

CHAPTER THREE

SPLASHES AND RIPPLES

Earlier, we mentioned the fact that our father, one day high in the mountains of Sanpete County, Utah, taught us about splashes and ripples, about our deeds and their effects upon ourselves and others. Now it is time to explore that concept more fully.

Some months ago we were rusticating at our family home in Fountain Green, Utah. We each spent a couple of hours reading a small paperback that had recently been given to us. It was titled *Return from Tomorrow* and was written by George G. Ritchie, M.D. (Grand Rapids, Michigan: Chosen Books, 1978.) We were so impressed with the spirit of the book that we began researching where we might locate the author, hoping that perhaps he would be able to visit with us.

One can imagine our elation and surprise when, with just two phone calls, we located Doctor Ritchie. He answered the phone himself, and even though he was just leaving his home for the evening, he graciously spent the next forty-five minutes visiting with us about his experience. He expressed his puzzlement that it seemed only Mormons were interested in his book, and that he had had more copies of the Book of Mormon presented to him than he could ever possibly read.

For us, it was a most delightful hour spent, one we will

long remember. And even though we do not recommend the book he wrote as doctrine, still we think his experience sheds light on a correct principle. Without tantalizing you further, let us share the premise of his book with you.

In the latter part of 1943, Dr. George G. Ritchie, then a young airman assigned to Camp Barkeley, Texas, contracted pneumonia and suffered what many choose to call a near-death experience. His spirit left his body, and he met with a glorious being of light who was identified to Ritchie as the Son of God. In a remarkable way he was shown much of mortality and immortality from a unique perspective.

At first young Ritchie was not even aware that he had "died." All he knew was that he had "lost his hardness" and that he was unable to get back into the body of the young man who wore his ring and who he was certain was himself. Then, as he recognized the futility of his efforts, he became aware of a light that was filling the tiny room. The light grew in brightness, and suddenly he realized that the light was not a light but a person who seemed literally to be made of light and glory. And in that same instant he saw his entire life. He describes that experience as follows:

> Every detail of twenty years of living was there to be looked at. The good, the bad, the high points, the run-of-the-mill. And with this all-inclusive view came a question. It was implicit in every scene and, like the scenes themselves, seemed to proceed from the [personage] beside me.
>
> *What did you do with your life?*
>
> It was obviously not a question in the sense that He was seeking information, for what I had done with my life was in plain view. In any case, this total recalling, detailed and perfect, came from Him, not me. I couldn't have remembered a tenth of what was there until He showed it to me.
>
> *What did you do with your life?*
>
> It seemed to be a question about values, not facts: what did you accomplish with the precious time you were allotted? And with this question shining through them, these ordinary events of a fairly typical boyhood seemed not merely unexciting but trivial. Hadn't I done anything lasting, any-

53

thing important? Desperately I looked around me for something that would seem worthwhile in the light of this [personage].

It wasn't that there were spectacular sins, just the sexual hang-ups and secretiveness of most teenagers. But if there were no horrendous depths, there were no heights either. Only an endless, shortsighted, clamorous concern for myself. Hadn't I ever gone beyond my own immediate interests, done anything other people would recognize as valuable? At last I located it, the proudest moment of my life:

"I became an Eagle Scout!"

Again, words seemed to emanate from the Presence beside me:

That glorified you.

It was true. I could see myself standing in the center of the award circle, flushed with pride, the admiring eyes of my family and friends turned on me. Me, me, me—always in the center. Wasn't there any time in my life when I had let someone else stand there? (Pp. 52-53.)

The amazing conversation continued, and the young man's foolish anger was shown and instantly rebuffed by a sort of joy and love that seemed like nothing so much as holy laughter, not mocking, but only loving. And then the question was there again before George Ritchie:

What have you done with your life to show Me?

Already I understood that in my first frantic efforts to come up with an impressive answer, I had missed the point altogether. He wasn't asking about accomplishments and awards.

The question, like everything else proceeding from Him, had to do with love. How much have you loved with your life? Have you loved others as I am loving you? Totally? Unconditionally?

Hearing the question like that, I saw how foolish it was even to try to find an answer in the scenes around us. Why, I hadn't known love like this was possible. Someone should have told me, I thought indignantly! A fine time to discover what life was all about—like coming to a final exam and discovering you were going to be tested on a subject you had never studied. If this was the point of everything, why hadn't someone told me?

But these thoughts rose out of self-pity and self-excuse, the answering thought held no rebuke, only that hint of heavenly laughter behind the words:

I did tell you.

But how? Still wanting to justify myself: how could He have told me and I not heard?

I told you by the life I lived. I told you by the death I died. And, if you keep your eyes on Me, you will see more. (Pp. 54-55.)

Dr. Ritchie went on to learn a great deal more about the ramifications of our actions during mortality, and we will come back to that. For now, however, let us reemphasize the message of the Being of Light: the whole point of going through this mortal probation is so that we can learn how to love and be loved; and *he showed us the way.* In the New Testament, he said it in this manner: "A new commandment I give unto you, That ye love one another; as I have loved you, that ye also love one another. By this shall all men know that ye are my disciples, if ye have love one to another." (John 13:34-35.)

Discipleship, which according to Christ is manifest by love, should be the goal of every human being. Of course, being human implies weakness and imperfection, and each of us suffers with that. Still, we are commanded to set ourselves the goal of perfection and to "walk uprightly" as we work toward it. Walking uprightly, or trying to do better in keeping the commandments of God, seems to be what being a disciple is all about. Therefore, in spite of our mortal weaknesses, discipleship can indeed become ours. Discipleship is the preventing of misery and the bringing of joy to other people. That is, it is love.

Now we know that, you and I. We want to change and do better in our relationships with others. Yet even with such lofty desires, the day-to-day realities of life, the ugliness, cruelty, lustfulness, selfishness, and even the simple busyness that assail us can dull our senses and thwart our desires so that our progress ceases and our direction is backward.

There are many reasons why we do or do not show love, and we discussed one of those in the chapter on competition. Now, rather than delve into further possible reasons for our inhumanity toward others, we will instead discuss what Dad called the "splash and ripple effect," an effect that circumvents all the reasons in the world.

When a stone is tossed into a pond, there is a splash, and then ripples go outward in all directions, and they would do so to infinity if all conditions were right. So too with our actions. There is never a time when what we do or think or say does not splash upon us, never a time when the ripples from our splashings do not affect other people, perhaps for generations to come. Interestingly, this is simply a ramification of Deutch's Law. Notice how that law applies to this illustration.

My parents were converted to the gospel when I was a baby, and when I was still very young we were sealed in the temple. We were happy and active in the Church, and everything seemed good. Then, shortly after my eighteenth birthday, things didn't seem so good any more. Confusion and contention settled into our home. Dad and Mom quarreled all the time, the rest of us got caught up in it, and things became progressively worse.

Of course, there had been hard times all along, with many serious illnesses and such things, but we had worked through them as a family and had grown stronger as a result. Now, however, it was different. No one was willing to work together, and finally my parents divorced.

But even that didn't end the bitterness. My parents and their respective attorneys fought bitterly and dishonestly over the properties, and my sister and I saw all of this corruption, especially as displayed by my father. There was no giving in him, and no compromise. He fought for every penny and made statements that made us not only lose respect for him, but stop loving him as well.

The effects were numerous. People in our ward stared at us. Some gossiped and some tried to console us, and we felt more isolated than ever. Even our family's close friends were no longer around, probably because we no longer had family interests like they did.

It was a nightmare I am still not over, for I think and think, why? Why the financial problems? Why was my parents' entire married life lived in vain? Of what point was the sealing in the temple? Since the divorce I have been constantly depressed. I never stop feeling guilty because somehow I think I might have stopped the hurt before it really got going, and my mind keeps asking, why the pain? Why the divorce? Why ever even try to have an eternal family?

The splash and ripple effect is very evident in that tragic situation. One or two people choose to turn from righteousness to follow selfish desires, making a splash, from which the ripples go out, damaging the children, affecting friends and associates, creating sorrow in the hearts of caring others, and on and on. First a splash, and then ripples that go out and out. Here is another example.

Since the day he was born, his father did not want him. On outings to the zoo, his father would sit in the car while his mother would show him the animals. If they were not back in the required time, his father would become angry and throw out the little boy's bottle of milk.

As he grew up, not a week went by where he did not get a swollen face or a whipping from his father's belt. Not an action or word of love came from his father. Instead, words of hate constantly bombarded the boy's life. "Get out of this house! You're nothing but the devil himself! You're good for nothing!"

In his teen years the boy could take it no longer. He retaliated, swore at his father, and even fought back physically. Then he would be kicked out and would be gone sometimes for weeks.

His mother attempted to do what she could, but it was not enough, and the boy gradually became inactive as he grew up. He is now a heavy drinker with the gospel totally foreign to his life.

This boy is my brother. My heart aches for him so much that I have taken his side. I respect and love him more than I can express, and I can hardly imagine what my father has done to this man who is still his son.

Isn't it sad how obvious and destructive these ripples are, the effects of our own selfish splashings in the pond of life?

I recall when my mother ran for a public office in our city. I was the only child left at home, and she desperately needed my help to distribute signs and help campaign. I thought, "Me distribute posters of my mother? I won't be caught dead doing such a thing. After all, somebody I know might recognize me!"

She even had me tie a large poster of her on top of my car, and I had to drive to college and all over town with that monstrosity showing. I was humiliated, and I lost no opportunity of letting her know it. Funny, but when she won, I thought it was "cool" for her to be my mom.

In George Ritchie's account of his near-death experience, he records that the Being of Light told him that the main purpose of a human being's life was to learn to love others. That was why He had lived; it was also why He had died.

With that in mind, how would you say the individuals in the above accounts are doing? Wouldn't you agree that some of them have great need to fear for their eternal lives?

The Being of Light took George Ritchie from one location to another upon the earth, showing him the inhabitants, both living and dead. He saw disembodied people chained to family and business situations from which they had never disengaged themselves during mortality. He saw others grasping and grappling without success for tobacco and alcohol and other substances, chained to earthly habits that their spirits could not partake of but could never stop craving.

He saw others in a constant state of unsuccessful apology to mortal beings; he was told that they were suicides, forever chained to every consequence of their act.

Ritchie asked the Being of Light why all this was so, why spirits did not just leave, and into his mind came the instant answer, "Lay not up for yourselves treasures upon earth—for where your treasure is, there will your heart be also." (See Matthew 6:19-21.)

Then Ritchie was given what was clearly his most eye-opening experience thus far. He writes:

> Although we were apparently still somewhere on the surface of the earth, I could see no living man or woman. The plain was crowded, even jammed with hordes of . . . discarnate beings. . . . All of these thousands of people were apparently no more substantial than I myself. And they were the most frustrated, the angriest, the most completely miserable beings I had ever laid eyes on.
>
> "Lord Jesus," I cried. "Where are we?"
>
> At first I thought we were looking at some great battlefield: everywhere people were locked in what looked like fights to the death, writhing, punching, gouging. It couldn't be a present day war because there were no tanks or guns. No weapons of any sort, I saw as I looked closer, only

bare hands and feet and teeth. And then I noticed that no one was . . . being injured. There was no blood, no bodies strewed the ground; a blow that ought to have eliminated an opponent would leave him exactly as before.

Although they appeared to be literally on top of each other, it was as though each man was boxing the air; at last I realized that of course, having no substance, they could not actually touch one another. They could not kill, though they clearly wanted to, because their intended victims were already dead, and so they hurled themselves at each other in a frenzy of impotent rage.

If I suspected before that I was seeing hell, now I was sure of it. Up to this moment the misery I had watched consisted in being chained to a physical world of which we were no longer part. Now I saw that there were other kinds of chains. Here were no solid objects or people to enthrall the soul. These creatures seemed locked into habits of mind and emotion, into hatred, lust, destructive thought-patterns.

Even more hideous than the bites and kicks they exchanged were the sexual abuses many were performing in feverish pantomime. Perversions I had never dreamed of were being vainly attempted all around us. It was impossible to tell if the howls of frustration which reached us were actual sounds or only the transference of despairing thoughts. Indeed in this disembodied world it didn't seem to matter. Whatever anyone thought, however fleetingly or unwillingly, was instantly apparent to all around him, more completely than words could have expressed it, faster than sound waves could have carried it.

And the thoughts most frequently communicated had to do with the superior knowledge, or abilities, or background of the thinker. "I told you so!" "I always knew!" "Didn't I warn you?" were shrieked into the echoing air over and over. With a feeling of sick familiarity I recognized here my own thinking. This was me, my very tone of voice—the righteous one, the award-winner, the churchgoer. At age twenty I hadn't yet developed any truly chaining physical habits, not like the beings I'd seen scrabbling to get close to that [alcohol or tobacco]. But in these yelps of envy and wounded self-importance I heard myself all too well.

Once again, however, no condemnation came from the [personage] at my side, only a compassion for these unhappy creatures that was breaking His heart. (Pp. 63-65.)

It is our prayer that we may understand the message of Dr. Ritchie's painful but informative experience. When we hurt others, intentionally or otherwise, the splash always comes back upon us, for justice is an eternal law; *unless we repent we will suffer.* And the further the ripples of suffering go out from our initial pain-causing action, the *more* we will need to suffer because of what we have caused.

However, we would be remiss if we explored only the dark side of this rippling effect. Let us bring the spotlight around to the other side and illuminate some beautiful and positive splashings and ripplings that we have observed.

We have a young friend named Steve who left this world on his twenty-second birthday. This was approximately one year ago, and yet still the impact of his ripples remains with us.

When Steve was a small child, he contracted muscular dystrophy, a disease that retards muscle and bone growth and leads to an early death. The family was at first in a state of shock, for not only did they see their entire family system affected, but they felt great pain that this bright, active son would not have the experiences of life that should have been his. Instead, he would be confined to a wheelchair, would become dependent on the care of his parents and brothers and sister, and would ultimately suffer a painful death.

As Steve's parents gathered strength and began to prayerfully and faithfully deal with this disease, many wonderful things occurred. First, they noticed that their own optimistic spirits were reflected by *each* of their children, including Steve. They then became creative with how they could adjust their own lives to make Steve's life more comfortable. This included building a home with an elevator so that Steve, in his wheelchair, could have access to both levels of their home. They then took great pride in purchasing a Volkswagen van so that he could be transported easily. They sacrificed and bought him an electric wheelchair, which they painted and supplied with lights, a built-in radio, extra padding—every convenience Steve and his family could imagine.

The magic of this family's enthusiasm for their son and his new way of life began to splash onto others. As he grew, Steve became one of the happiest, most popular young men in his school. He was involved in his school's activities and even ran for student-body office his senior year. Brenton spoke at Steve's seminary graduation, and as the other classmates worked their way around him on the stage of the Provo Tabernacle, it became apparent Steve was the true example and leader of his class.

Time passed, Steve's body weakened, and still he influenced others for good. With the help of his family, he completed his studies at Brigham Young University, and did so with distinction. Even more important, he prepared for the Melchizedek priesthood, received his endowments, and served regularly in the Provo Temple.

It seemed only appropriate that Steve desired to spend his twenty-second birthday with his family in the temple. They graciously complied with his request, and it was but a short time after returning home that evening that Steve bade his family farewell. Quietly then, with a smile born of righteous ripples, this dear friend slipped out of his small body, stretched his spiritual limbs for a moment, and then eagerly departed for his mission assignment in the world of spirits.

In contrast, we have another friend who had many emotional problems. Listen to his own description of what happened to him.

> There I was sitting in a nowhere scene. No one cared about me, and I didn't care about anyone— anyone, that is, except me. I was fed up with everything: school, church, people, myself, and, most of all, life.

Sure I'd always been active in church and school. I was a 100-percent attender at all my meetings, an honor student, and captain of the track team. I was also in band and choir. So what? Who cared about me?

I tried all sorts of escapes, but nothing gave me what I wanted—love. I did the best I could to hide myself from this lack of love, but I was going nowhere—except maybe to hell. But who even cared about that? I hated myself, life, and my peers, who were ever so righteous. Why didn't any of them care about me?

I still read the scriptures to please Mommy and Daddy and all the seminary teachers, but it just seemed that I delved deeper into a sea of hypocrisy. I just couldn't feel what I was reading. But no matter. I wasn't worth saving anyway. Suicide seemed the answer, but the consequences made it not worth the trouble.

Then one day, as I was dreaming of my own annihilation, some sickly-sweet girl sat beside me in history.

"Hi there."

"Hi." *Who, me? Sure, sister. Sure.* I turned away and didn't think much more about the incident until the next day.

"Good morning. Do you mind if I sit here again?"

"Go ahead." *What is she, crazy? What's a celestial girl like her sitting by me for? She probably needs glasses. Either that, or she's a lot dumber than she looks.*

I don't know how she did it, but the next Tuesday she got me talking. Not talking, really. I mostly listened and nodded in agreement every once in a while. It was amazing. I hadn't talked with anyone for that long about anything—ever! *The poor girl must be crazy, thinking I'm worthwhile enough to talk to.*

After a few weeks I found myself looking forward

63

to history. Me—the person who had always cared about nothing. It began to worry me. How could I feel sorry for myself if someone else thought I was okay? That settled it. She was bonkers, and I would pay her no more attention.

It was on Friday before Christmas—my least favorite time of year. Everyone was singing about love, peace, and happiness—it must be something in the snow, I decided. Anyway, school had just let out, and I was looking forward to getting wasted.

"Hey, wait a minute!" shouted a voice from behind me.

There she was, all red-faced, breathless, and smiling. "I have something for you," she said. "Merry Christmas."

Before I realized it, she'd slipped a package into my hands and was on her bus, heading home.

I waved at a window that I hoped was hers, said thanks, and tried to smile.

I got home straight—I decided to give up the wasting—and sat down on my bed to open the package, still marveling. Still, I figured it was a copy of the Book of Mormon. They were all the same, those good LDS girls. I tore off a corner, just to be sure. Yep. There was the old familiar blue. I knew it. However, I guessed I might as well open it, so I did, expecting any minute to see ol' Moroni smiling at me from the cover.

But there wasn't any Moroni; there wasn't even a Book of Mormon. There was just a small blue box—full of something. I hurriedly opened it to see, and found a mirror and a note. I pulled a few faces at the mirror, and then read the note.

"Dear Mike," she began, "I've thought about it a lot, and I've even prayed about it. And the best thing I could give you for Christmas is yourself. I know you've told me what you think about you, but I see something more than nothing. Mike, I see a child of God. Not a Junior Sunday School child of God, but a prince of the kingdom, just two steps or so from Godhood. Mike, I believe in you. Each morning when you get up, look in this mirror and say to yourself, 'I am a child of God,' and remember it. *For as a man thinketh in his heart, so is he.* Merry Christmas, Mike. May God bless you. Love, Linda."

I picked up the mirror and said to it, half in jest, "Mike, you are a child of God." Suddenly I felt funny inside. "I believe in you," she had said. "Two steps from Godhood."

That afternoon I went to the store to buy Linda a Christmas card. Maybe there's something in the snow that changes people, I don't know. But I felt that it was the least I could do for someone who believed in me. After all, I was a son of God, a prince of his kingdom.

At times we jump into the pond of someone's life and make a large and powerfully painful splash. Then, just as we are going under the water, we realize what we have done. At such a crucial moment, the best thing we can do is get out of the water quickly, turn ourselves around, and jump back in at the right angle, or, in other words, with a joyful and giving splash of repentance. To illustrate:

In 1960 while working on my master's degree at Indiana University, I had Dr. Karl Bookwalter as one of my instructors. He was an outstanding teacher, active in Boy Scout work, and a well-known author of textbooks. He was also a fierce-looking person, with a very gruff voice who had half of the graduate students in his class scared to death of him.

As a young teacher in the Denver area many years before, Dr. Bookwalter had taught health and physical-education courses. At that time it had been customary in the gym classes to conduct health inspections on the students in relation to personal hygiene, general health, physical development, and so on.

During one of these inspections, Dr. Bookwalter found one boy who had extremely dirty feet. He was berated by the professor publicly, as the professor said, "You have the dirtiest feet that I have ever seen on a human!" and sent him into the showers to take care of his problem.

When Dr. Bookwalter went into the locker room after the class was over, the boy was sitting in the corner, crying. As the professor approached, the boy slowly looked up and showed him the shoe he was holding in his hand. In the sole was a hole big enough to put his hand through, with a layer of badly worn cardboard being used as an inner-sole to cover up the hole. He softly said, "Sir, do you know why my feet were dirty? These are the only shoes I have, and when they're gone I don't know where I'm going to get any more."

There was little Dr. Bookwalter could say after this quiet speech, but the next day there was a new pair of shoes in the boy's locker when he came to class.

Dr. Bookwalter told this story as a lesson to his students to always be sure they knew the full story before they chastised someone. It was a good lesson for that, but it was also a lesson about someone who cared about another individual. There were many wet eyes in the classroom the day this story was told, and together we saw a new side of this crusty old professor.

Read now another true story of a young woman who jumped into life from the wrong angle, but who was quickly washed over by ripples of kindness from another person's splash, and so was able to repent and get on with her eternal progression.

I yawned sleepily as the girls and I climbed out of the car. What a way to spend a Saturday. As we stood dumbfounded in our old work clothes, our advisor promised us rich rewards. "Yeah," I thought, "sore muscles and dirty fingernails."

Soon we were on our hands and knees pulling weeds. The morning was beautiful, and soon we were all laughing and joking, thanks to an enthusiastic advisor.

Every so often Sister Castanzo would come over to the door and smile at us through the screen. She was a quiet lady whom we rarely saw at church—a widow living all alone in her little yellow house. It seemed that whenever the Mutual had to do a service project, it always involved Sister Castanzo.

After we had worked all morning, her yard was finally in tip-top shape. As we put away our tools, out came Sister Castanzo with cool lemonade and coconut macaroons. I hate coconut macaroons, but I ate one just to be polite. I then climbed into my car, repining over my wasted Saturday.

A month later our family was trying to think of something to do for someone on Thanksgiving day. I remembered Sister Castanzo, and although I really didn't want to spend my Thanksgiving working, I knew I had to, and I knew that she would accept our help. So I suggested we rake her leaves.

It was a beautiful, crisp morning when our family appeared at her house. Sister Castanzo was surprised yet very delighted to see us. We raked and weeded, cleaned her yard, and then played in the pile of leaves we had gathered. I was actually beginning to enjoy myself.

When we finished, out of the house struggled this dear old lady. Again she thanked us, only this time she invited us into her home. We wiped the leaves from our clothes and followed her into the living room.

Sister Castanzo's home was very clean, and it was filled with knick-knacks. We were all very impressed with her doll collection. She told us about her family and showed us pictures of her only child, a son, who had died in the war. This woman, for years, had been completely alone.

As we visited, I began to realize that this was not just some helpless old lady, nice to have around for service projects, but that she was a gentle, kind human being with special needs and gifts to give others.

As you can guess, out came the lemonade and the coconut macaroons. I'll have to admit, too, that I have never tasted such good macaroons!

It is interesting to observe others, especially those who enjoy being observed as they attempt to make giant, obtrusive splashes in life. As Jesus said, they have their reward. Then there are others, true disciples, who seek to shun the limelight and yet whose splashings and ripples are spreading, affecting the lives of many. We would like to tell you about one such man, a brother to some very dear friends of ours, Owen and Charlotte. It is their son who relates the following story and who is among those who have felt the ripples of that man's life.

During my short life I have been privileged to witness a great many acts of caring shown by my Uncle Paul. He has recently become active in the Church, returned to the temple after many years of absence, and is now serving as president of the elders quorum in his ward. He was always a good, honest, hardworking man, but one who spent many years outside the bosom of the Church.

Regardless of his Church activity, Paul has always been concerned about the welfare of his neighbors, and he has been the first in line to help when there was a need. His farming experience and expertise were always used at harvest or planting time at the ward welfare farm. He donated time and machinery each year to keep the ward farm in A-1 condition. He has served the community as watermaster and has been on the sheriff's possee.

As elders quorum president, he has assumed responsibility for the widows of the ward in addition to his other responsibilities. He checks to insure that the widows' heating supplies are adequate, that their walks are shoveled in the winter, and that their lawns are cared for in the summer, and he makes sure they have transportation to meetings and appointments. In addition, each spring he plows and prepares their garden plots. These acts of caring are done quietly and without fanfare, with never a thought of repayment or notice.

Paul loves young people and children, and whenever any of his grandchildren, nieces, or nephews are around, he sweeps them up and takes them along on his tractor or takes them to help feed his cattle, irrigate the field, or whatever other task he is doing.

His caring acts even include planting a special area of his farm in corn to entice a pheasant crop to be used by his family at pheasant-hunting time. The crop is never harvested but is solely for his family's fall hunting needs.

Paul's caring also extends to animals, and especially to his German shepherd, Sugar, who is his constant companion and who occupies a seat next to him in his truck. In addition, each of his baby beef know of his kindness and stand to be scratched on the forehead by him. He takes pride in beautiful, healthy stock.

The culminating example of Paul's caring occurred about two years ago. There was a young man in the ward who had prepared for a mission. Coming from a farm background where money was not always in abundance, the family were feeling a hardship in keeping the boy supplied with what he needed in the mission field. This faithful family, nevertheless, did all that was necessary to provide for this young man who was serving the Lord.

About that time, Paul and several others in the ward decided they wanted to help support this missionary with monthly contributions. When they approached the boy's parents, the parents considered it an answer to their prayers. The money was faithfully sent to the missionary each month, and even when the others were unable to donate, the needed funds were provided entirely by Paul. This unselfish act became known when the boy's parents came to my father and told of Paul's quiet act of caring. I surely do love that uncle, and I just hope that when I am able to help others, it will be quietly and without fanfare, just as he has done.

Most often, when our ripples of discipleship do the most good, they are caused by splashes we are not even aware we have made. Let us conclude this chapter by sharing three examples of this, each having to do with young people who are concerned with becoming true disciples of our Savior.

While I was in high school, I had a lot of friends. Still, there were many others I just didn't care about. They sort of existed, but we never spoke to each other unless we were forced into a situation where it was necessary.

Then one day, when I was walking down the hallway with my friend, I received quite a jolt. A lot of different people would walk by and say hi to my friend, people who were total strangers to me, and many of them would stop and talk to her, laughing and joking and just having a good time.

I continued to wonder about this friend as we would go to a dance, a movie, or a game. She seemed to know everyone, and others were always saving us good seats, or would always ask her to dance. Even people she didn't know would walk up to her and say, "Aren't you so and so?" And she would say, "Yes. How do you know me?" And they would usually answer, "Oh, I know so and so, and he or she knows you."

Constantly I wondered why others wanted so badly to be her friend. She wasn't that much cuter than I was. I tried to be nice to others, and I definitely wasn't stuck up. So what was the difference? I thought maybe she made exciting conversations, or that perhaps she was an excellent speaker. But as I watched her, I finally discovered the difference between her and me.

My friend really *cared* about people. When they told her about their problems, she didn't just say, "Oh, that's too bad," and then do nothing about it. She really cared and showed sincere concern. She made every person she knew feel as if they were really important, as if everything they said and did meant something special to her. She just didn't act this way toward people she was close to, but she treated even the ones who just "existed" in my life as very special to her.

As teachers, we have had dozens of students bemoan to us their lack of friends. When that happens, and it still occasionally does, we tell them of the young lady in that story, who has discovered the key to becoming.

Quite inadvertantly, the young man who relates the following experience also discovered it.

I first met Tim in junior high. He was beginning seventh grade, and I was just entering ninth grade. I had no idea what kind of impact this small, freckle-faced redhead would have on my life.

As an athlete, I was fairly popular all through my

junior-high years. Many people thought of athletes as stuck-up jocks. Those people didn't realize how close people can become through sports.

The basketball season was just beginning when I first came in contact with Tim. His father, concerned for his son, came to me and asked me to help Tim. I agreed, because Tim was fun to be around, and I enjoyed working with other people.

Later in the year, Tim became one of the few seventh graders to make the baseball team, playing my backup as shortstop. I remembered what it was like when I was a seventh grader on the school team: the older guys resented me. That was a miserable experience, and I didn't want Tim to go through such a thing. He was really shy, but with a little bit of teasing Tim opened up and became one of the guys.

My senior year was the best year of my life. I had fun in every way possible. At the end of the year I also learned what it means to a younger person to have someone older show interest in him. It was a hard way to learn this, but I am so glad I had been lucky enough to do it.

Tim and I played opposite each other in basketball practices; we played beside each other in baseball when I switched from shortstop to third; and the other guys and I went out of our way to let Tim and the one or two other younger players know they weren't just sophomores but were important players to us. What we did wasn't all that great, but I guess that little things seem bigger when they are needed and appreciated.

Then one night a man trying to commit suicide slammed into Tim and his dad's car at over ninety miles an hour. Tim's dad escaped with a broken arm and leg, but Tim was killed instantly.

I didn't know what to do, so I went to the hospital to see Tim's father. What he told me really affected me. He said, "I know I'll miss Tim more than anything in the world, but I know I've had sixteen beautiful years with my son. There are a lot of fathers who wish they could say that, and their kids are adults." He went on to tell me what it meant to a young athlete to have an older guy watch out for him, like I guess I had been doing for Tim. I hadn't thought of it until then, for Tim hadn't been a "younger kid" to me at all. He had only been my friend.

I thought about Tim's father's thanks to me for a long time, and it seems to me now that it ought to be Tim who is thanked, not me. Tim was the one who made caring so easy, for his family, for me, and for everyone else he knew.

And now a final account. This young man's experience started out normally enough, and was probably motivated by typically selfish, or at least self-seeking, desires. But as the experience unfolded, so did the young man's good character, and he ended up sending out some truly eternal ripples of caring. Imagine how many, across the spans of forever, will be affected by them.

Last summer I met the most spectacular-looking girl I have ever seen. She was incredibly beautiful, and she would have melted the heart of any typical red-blooded American male. She surely melted mine. Actually, she was perfect in all aspects except one: she had no moral standards.

She was very popular and went out constantly. But she was involved with all her dates in drinking and all else that seemed to go with it, and I guess she had given up hope of ever being the kind of woman that deep inside herself she really wanted to be.

I met her on a blind date and went out of my head over her. Afterward we went to my apartment for a bite to eat. I hadn't heard anything about her, so I thought everything about her was wonderful.

The next day, however, I started hearing all sorts of things about her, and the more I heard, the worse I felt.

Finally I prayed about what I was feeling, and then I called her up and invited her to church. She accepted. Sunday came, and as I drove to her home I prayed that she would feel the Lord's Spirit that day and would begin to believe in herself. When she opened the door, she stood there as a vision of beauty, all in white, and I knew then that she could become pure if she would just believe in her ability to repent and in the Lord's power of forgiveness.

Our sacrament service was fast and testimony meeting, and the Spirit of the Lord was there in great power and strength. I felt it, my date felt it (and cried through the entire meeting), and I think everyone there must have felt it too. Afterward we talked for several hours, and she was so impressed with the Church and the members and even more impressed with the warmth that she had felt from the Spirit of the Lord.

Later I took her home, and she thanked me for the date. Then, in a subdued voice, she told me it was the first time she had ever been out with a guy where she knew she would not have to have relations with him. Then she thanked me for caring enough to treat her like a lady, and she told me she was going to get more involved with the Lord.

When I walked away from her that night, all I could think of was my gratitude to God for all the righteous truths I had been taught by my parents and teachers throughout my life. I can't even express how good I felt, but it was great!

Since then this girl has been baptized and is a happy, pure, sweet daughter of God. She and I are close friends, and I will always be thankful that Heavenly Father let me be a small part of her becoming a disciple of the Lord.

CHAPTER FOUR

ON TILT

A year or so ago, while serving as a bishop, Brent made the following entry in his journal:

I recently had an impression regarding sin that keeps sticking to my spiritual ribs. I haven't read of this insight before, though it feels like one of those promised "doctrines of the priesthood" that will, as we need them, distill upon our souls as dews from heaven.

In considering personal sin and the repentance process, there is a natural and expected "standard" way of seeking repentance for a sin committed. That is, if we are on tilt we are admonished to forsake our wrongdoing, confess it to our bishop, and then righteously study and pray the effects of the sin out of our spiritual fabric.

As bishop, it has been my experience that many people choose not to complete this repentance loop but merely comply with the first two phases. That is, they stop doing that which is wrong, and then appropriately confess it. They then recite a couple of prayers and are on their way, which leaves the Lord with no option other than to allow that person to continue to suffer with guilt or anxiety or frustration.

These feelings of guilt seem to cause a person to

then interact with others *defensively*. That is, they project their spiritual discomfort by letting others know how "out to lunch" and unsupportive they are of that individual. The unrepentant person spends his time lashing out at others, simply to remove the heat from his own misbehavior. Thus, those around this person become unwitting whipping posts.

As we contemplate the process of becoming a disciple of Jesus Christ, we discover that many of God's children do not seem to know the way back from their spiritual tilt. That is, their lives are not upright according to God's definition of righteousness, and they do not know what to do about it.

Strangely, many of these people believe they are right, and others spend their time trying to convince themselves that they are. This is not only an exercise in futility, but it has an amazing negative impact on people who are associated with these "on tilt" individuals.

The following accounts, while tragic, illustrate how devastating such associations (ripples) can be.

It was in December that my father moved out of our home, finally being unable to contain his guilty feelings about the way he had been conducting his life. It was then that we saw how he had completely fallen away from the Church. He had been active until he couldn't live a double standard any longer, and he told my mother he had been unfaithful to her.

I have never seen anyone go through the great suffering that my mother went through in the weeks and months to follow. The most awful part of it was that my father did not want to correct his life. He was vice-president of a good company and could afford to live very well, and he wanted to continue his immoral life.

At first I was able to handle my emotions quite

well. I suppose it was because I was in shock or thought that what was happening was just a bad dream. I was able to comfort my mother and was there for her to gain support from.

The reservoir of my emotions kept filling up, though, and finally the dam burst! I couldn't deal with my emotions in front of my mother, simply because I was her pillar. So I called my Laurel advisor, went to her home, and then spent an entire evening pouring out my heart to her.

I will always remember how this beautiful, understanding woman listened attentively until I got the entire load off my chest. Then, without speaking, she just held me in her arms while I cried my tears away. She then talked to me and told me the things she felt would help me with the trials that awaited our family.

As time passed, life became an even greater nightmare. My father, having moved out, completely stopped contact with us for a full month. He was going through his own suffering during this time. My mother, her emotions now drained, was not able to function in any area of her life. She was just trying to survive this period of time. As a result, many extra responsibilities of our family fell upon my shoulders.

Looking back, I can see how badly this situation affected me as well. I felt estranged from my closest friends, and their awkwardness caused the gap in our friendship to widen daily. I was taking an extra-heavy load in school, and I watched my 3.8 grade point average plunge drastically. It was then that I was tested as I have never before or since been tested. I knew I was alone, completely alone. I would pray fervently for my Heavenly Father to help me, but still things became worse.

The only things I had to rely upon during that

time were my testimony, my patriarchal blessing, and my Laurel advisor, Marty. She made herself available to me whenever I needed to talk or just to be with someone. Sometimes we would go shopping together, and she would be the friend I so badly needed.

There were times when the loss of my precious family would really get to me. I would look at my father and ask myself, "Is it all worth it, just to live the gospel of Jesus Christ?" At that time the gospel seemed like just another intruding pressure. It seemed to me it would be so much easier for us all to give up and give in to the standards of the world. At least we would be a happy family again.

It was during these doubting moments that Marty would sense my struggles and come daily to my aid. As I became closer to her, Marty's husband became a friend as well. He became a role model, and he really showed he cared by talking to me and giving me support and counsel. He never did mind my being in his home, but instead he helped me to feel like part of his family.

Then came the day when I felt I could not take life's pressures another hour. I felt totally alone, at a loss as to where to turn. I went to Marty's home and received a special blessing from her husband. It was after that blessing that I knew things would work out, and that God did live, and did love me.

Now, years later, I find myself able to cope with what has happened. I still ache for my family to be as it once was, but I know that agency is what life is all about and that I can't force my father to be who he does not want to be. I know also that I will always be his daughter, and that I should love him regardless of his actions. After all, in spite of the divorce, this is what my mother has done, and it is exactly what Marty and her husband taught me to do.

Perhaps one of the darkest and yet most pressing problems within the Church today is that of physical and sexual abuse. As does everyone else, we feel a great reluctance in discussing this epidemic moral disease. Nevertheless, members of the Church everywhere are being swept over and even drowned by the splashes and ripples of this truly satanic behavior.

But rather than considering the sin of abuse itself, which is handled very aptly by President Spencer W. Kimball in his book *The Miracle of Forgiveness*, it is our desire to show the ramifications of this sin by those who are on tilt, the ripples if you will, upon the lives of other people.

My home may not be broken, but it sure is cracked! The main problem is my father, who feels that the only way to teach his children is to beat them mercilessly. For as long as I can remember, my father has used his belt to solve all problems, big or small. As a result, my older brother left home before he was sixteen.

After seeing the hassle he went through, the rest of us played the "Let's avoid Dad game." If you avoid a person long enough, any love that existed will soon die. And it doesn't take much to turn a dead love into hate, either. That's what happened to us. My youngest sister, who felt the leather lash often because she dared stand up to him, won't even call him father.

There was finally a divorce. Then my father tried to pay more attention to us, he and mother remarried, and our friendship with him might have improved except that he had taught us too well. How can you learn to love someone if all you have ever received from him is anger and hatred?

So now, with each of us grown and married, there is almost no desire in any of us to remain a family. The others have even fallen away from activity in the Church. My husband and I visited with our bishop about it, and he told us just that we should be a strength to them without being critical. We are trying to do this, and even though it is a long and mostly unrewarding experience, there are occasional rays of light with my brothers and sisters.

With my father, unfortunately, there are none. My hatred for him and what he has done to all of us has become so consuming that I think I must subconsciously feel that if he were dead, everything would be okay. I dream, at least once a month, about killing him. Last night was an example, but I do not care to describe it. I am scared of those dreams, pray that they will stop, and pray too for the power to forgive my father for the evil he has done.

Talk about splashes and ripples of evil! Is it any wonder that the scriptures declare that any man who does not care for his family denies the faith and is worse than an infidel? (1 Timothy 5:8.) But this great evil is found not only within families. Any time a man or woman exercises unjust power over another human being, any time an individual selfishly seeks to take virtue from another, that individual has denied the faith of God and can no longer have the companionship of the Holy Ghost.

Consider this example:

It all began four years ago. I was a college student, a member of my sorority, an employee of a department store, and yet I had not dated a great deal to that point. Therefore, I was not prepared for what happened next.

While back in the stockroom unloading shelves, I was approached by my department manager. We were discussing pricing procedures, when all of a sudden he grabbed me and embraced me. After a few moments he let go and told me I had better get back out on the sales floor, to which I readily agreed.

I realize now that I should have been appalled or

scared or something; but I wasn't. In fact, to the contrary I was really kind of overwhelmed and excited. It was nice to think that a man was attracted to me, and not just as a friend. After all, Steve (as I shall call him) was handsome, a sharp dresser, very intelligent, and an excellent manager. I had always felt a great respect for him and enjoyed working for him.

Steve sought me out many times after that day. He wanted me to respond to his embraces by kissing him, but somehow I just couldn't. I resisted for almost a year. (Now you might feel that I was being unfair, but there was another side to Steve. You see, he was married, and it was his second marriage, at that.)

Then one day Steve caught me in the stockroom. My guard was down, and this time when he tried to kiss me, he succeeded. It was then that I learned the truth in the statement that "sin becomes easier the second time, and even easier the next."

It was not long before Steve wasn't satisfied with just a kiss. He wanted more. I knew what I was doing was wrong, but somehow I was caught on a merry-go-round, and I couldn't get off. I also knew I was in the middle of destroying another family, and I knew the Lord did not bless relationships that are inappropriate. Yet still I continued. The emotional fulfillment he provided seemed to at least partially fill a void that had been forever in my heart.

Steve knew his ways with women, and soon I found myself doing things I never really believed possible. We weren't together often, but he wasted no time when we were. If I needed a ride home from work, Steve set conditions that I had to "play." If I refused to go along with his whims, there was the story of how his wife didn't love him and wouldn't have relations with him. Constantly he reminded me that his marriage wouldn't last, but that it was not my fault. He even asked me if I would consider marrying him after he was divorced. But the thing that affected me the most was when he would begin crying and then beg me to submit.

I didn't know what to do. I had no one to turn to, and I was going crazy. I knew now, more than ever, that I had to do something or I would destroy myself. I cried myself to sleep each night because of the torment that was churning in my soul. Finally, one night as I lay weeping in my room, I decided the only route left was to pray. And so I knelt down and prayed as I never had before, and with great humility and repentance. During the prayer I told the Lord that the burden I carried was too great, and that I knew he would not test me beyond my ability to resist. Even so, I told him if this temptation were not removed immediately, I would break. And then I became specific. I prayed that the Lord would transfer Steve to another store.

The next day, when I arrived at work, I witnessed a true miracle. The store's regional manager came in unexpectedly and informed the entire group of employees that Steve had been promoted, and that he had also been transferred.

Looking back, it was strange how everyone was shocked and surprised with Steve's transfer— everyone, that is, except me. I knew the entire occurrence had taken place as an answer to my prayer.

I will always be thankful that, in spite of my weaknesses, God heard my pleas and answered them. I will also be forever grateful that I did not allow Steve full intimacy, regardless of his pleadings.

Think of the terrible burden of responsibility that this man carries. He did as much as he was able to deprive a fair daughter of God of her chastity and virtue, which the prophet Moroni declared was most dear and precious above all things. Fortunately she turned to the Lord before she and the man had gone too far, and the Lord immediately responded. But that man, unless he repents, will remain accountable and must one day suffer, perhaps on the very plane of misery and despair that was shown to Dr. George Ritchie.

Frequently, however, people are not so fortunate as that young woman. They do *not* turn to the Lord, and so they have immoral experiences, even grossly so, as the prophet Jacob terms them. Then tremendous damage is done, and tremendous responsibility must be shouldered. We include the following account to illustrate that. But even more importantly, we hope to show a way of reacting to the problem or damage that we think is both healthy and refreshing. Would that all of us could be so loving and so forgiving.

My oldest sister has always been mature both physically and emotionally. When she was seventeen, after high-school graduation, she moved to Salt Lake City to try life on her own.

She found a job almost immediately. This sister had never been known for confiding much of anything, so when the letters started coming, the classic "everything is just fine" was in every line. The phone calls were many, and it was obvious at times that she was lonely, but not alarmingly so.

My sister had been gone eight months when it became apparent that she was having a financial crisis. My parents left on Friday morning, drove all the way to Salt Lake, and moved my sister home by Sunday. Still, none of us knew what her problems really were.

However, she made an immediate appointment with our bishop, and minutes before she was to leave, she confided to us that she was four months pregnant.

I can't remember if we asked the usual questions about the father and marriage. I do remember crying and thinking, "What have I done that caused this? What could I have done to prevent it?"

It was determined almost immediately that my sister would not marry and that she preferred to stay at home, if we would let her. It did cross our minds to have her live with some friends, but Dad pointed out that she could have stayed in Salt Lake City and we would have been oblivious to the whole situation. More than anything, we wanted my sister to know of our deep love for her, and so she stayed with us.

The tears were many. Very quickly she became noticeably pregnant, and it was hard for her. Yet the outpouring of love from our bishop and the other ward members was tremendous. Nothing like this had ever happened before in our ward. Yet everyone handled it well.

For months we had been having conversations as to the possible name for the baby, and several in the ward had promised to hold a shower for her so she would have things for the child. And then my dad mentioned that my sister ought to consider putting the baby up for adoption. We were all stunned. But my sister's reaction was only momentary.

Adoption. She became quiet and very prayerful about what her decision would be. Finally she decided that it was right for her to relinquish the baby. And the topic of a name for the child was never brought up again. The baby was always talked about in terms of being someone else's child, and my sister felt good about that.

A little girl was born, probably the prettiest baby I have ever seen. Two days later we said good-bye to the tiny infant and promised that we would never forget her, and then my sister handed her baby over to the Social Services.

Hard? It was devastating! We have shed many

tears while wondering how the baby was and if her new mom and dad loved her. But my sister kept up her courage, her self-pride, and her faith that Heavenly Father loved her, and she knew that she was doing the best thing she could do.

It has been over a year since my family shared this experience together, and we have learned much. Family relationships have become so much more important to all of us. We better understand the role of a bishop in repentance, and we have all learned how much we love my sister. We are so proud that she has blessed our home; we are strengthened by her testimony, her courage, and her love for the gospel of Jesus Christ, and we are thrilled with the sweet attitude she developed through her experience with repentance.

And now, with that reluctance we discussed earlier, we are going to share another experience that is tragically not unique among families, including those who have the gospel. This true account is most sensitive, and so you should be careful about the circumstances under which children read it. We include it in the hope that the signs of such abuse may be recognized and dealt with in other homes so that such tragedies can be avoided.

Every little girl needs to know how special she is, and at the age of three I was no different. I wanted to be happy, but I can remember that more than anything I wanted to make everyone around me happy, especially members of my family.

We lived in New York in a very small apartment. Living with us at that time were my grandparents. My twin sister and I slept in the "big" bedroom and thought it was neat. My parents slept in a small room off the bedroom, and my grandparents slept in the living room.

Late afternoons and early evenings were always

busy times with my mother and grandmother fixing dinner. It was fun watching them work in our tiny kitchen. When both my sister and I were with them, the kitchen seemed to get smaller, and everyone's patience got shorter.

Just about this time my grandfather would come home. He always came in with a smile, greeted everyone, took my hand, and told me how happy he was to see his special girl. I knew I made him happy because he would smile.

Then grandfather would take me out of that busy kitchen. We would go into the living room and close the door, and I knew that he would tell me one of his stories. It was just me and him—oh, how every little girl dreams of having a time, all by herself, with her grandpa.

Then things would start that I wouldn't quite understand. All I knew was that my grandfather was happy, and that I was the reason why. But my little mind couldn't comprehend how making someone happy—as he said I did—could make me hurt so much inside and out.

My grandfather would go over to where my father would keep his special little bottles, and he would have a drink of something that smelled awful. Then he would take me over to our special chair, and he would lift me high in the air and then set me on his lap. Sometimes he would start singing me songs, while other times he would tell me a story. But all the time this was going on, he would be touching me, and I would get so scared. I guess my eyes would show how scared I was, because he would then begin telling me how special I was, and how good a girl I was for making him so happy. He would also say that we shouldn't tell anyone else about our "special time" together because they might want to share it with us, and then there would be too many people around. Because I wanted my grandfather to be happy, I didn't tell anyone.

As I got older, I found myself hating the time when my grandfather would come home. My mind was getting so mixed up, and I didn't know what was right. Then my father lost his job, and I got sick and had to go to the hospital. I didn't want to go, but I was relieved because I would be away from my grandfather.

When I came home, I found out we were moving to California. I was probably the happiest one in the family, because my mother told me that my grandparents wouldn't be moving with us. Two years later, however, they moved west to be with us again, and I remember going into the backyard and holding my dog and crying. I was so afraid, and I was also experiencing a new feeling—*hatred.*

From the time my grandparents arrived, I lived with great fear. I found myself hiding in my room, making excuses to leave the house, and being very nasty any time I thought I would be alone with my grandfather. This fear continued until I was fourteen, when my father asked my grandparents to move out.

Finally I decided that my secret was safe. No one would ever know, and I would never have to worry about it again. But I was so wrong. For the next twenty-five years I blamed myself for what had happened. During this time I fell in love with and married the most gentle and understanding man. Our life together has been rich and filled with a deep love, but I could never understand how he could love me. My self-esteem was one big zero.

Eight years after we were married, I joined my husband's church: I became a Latter-day Saint. The happiness and joy of the gospel helped to make our home peaceful, and I felt I was happy.

Twenty-seven years after the nightmare began, my grandfather passed away. I remember attending his funeral and thinking, "It's all over." But only the fear had gone, not the hatred—hatred for him, and hatred for myself.

It's ironic how things work out for good if we but exercise patience and live righteously. Years later I was called to be a seminary teacher. In preparing the many lessons for my early morning class, it seemed that always the lessons were about forgiveness and charity, the pure love of Christ. Those lessons seemed to bring into the classroom a stronger presence of the Spirit, and I would leave feeling a little different and would wonder why.

Finally one day I knew the answer. For all these years my heart had been filled with such hatred for my grandfather that I couldn't forgive him. Thus, I couldn't be forgiven of my hatred, and I didn't have the Spirit with me, either. What was I to do?

I knew I had to tell someone, and the only one I could think of was my husband. It wasn't easy explaining to the man I love the horrible events that had taken place. I felt terribly ashamed. But he was wonderful. There wasn't any judging—he just loved me. That was when I knew I needed to love my grandfather—really love him if I was to forgive him.

I prayed and worked hard, and I could feel a softening of my heart. Then one day I had an overwhelming desire to do my grandparents' temple work. What a joyous day, for then I knew that complete forgiveness was there, and my heart was filled only with compassion and love for him.

A couple of months later my husband and I were able to go to the temple, kneel across the altar from each other, and have my grandparents sealed for time and all eternity. My husband kissed me across the altar, and I felt an overwhelming feeling that my grandfather had been forgiven by the Lord, and that he and my grandmother were with us, rejoicing.

Now I realize that I was not responsible at all for my grandfather's actions. I was only a little girl, completely innocent. I now know that I am a daughter of God, and that God has loved me since the very beginning of my life.

So many times, children unnecessarily carry into adult-hood this terrible burden of guilt. For years, sometimes throughout mortality, this guilt robs them of their ability to love others because they cannot love themselves. Imagine the terrible burden the one who has caused that guilt will carry. When Dr. Ritchie saw the disembodied people locked in fruitless battles and feverish but ineffective pantomimes of lust upon that great and miserable spirit plain, it is no wonder that they howled so miserably. To pay for such Satan-pleasing misery as they have caused in mortality will take more suffering, we suppose, than any of us would ever want to experience.

Thank God above that Christ cared enough to suffer, thus giving us the opportunity to repent and so avoid those horrors described by Dr. Ritchie and many, many of the an-cient and modern prophets. Oh, if only we will forsake that evil.

While we do not intend to share any specific examples of spouse abuse, let us not forget that it is just as evil as child abuse, and that the damage created in the spirit of the hus-band or wife so abused can be just as long-lasting and devas-tating.

When a man and woman marry, they begin a partner-ship in which each of them works with the other to bring about mutual happiness. No marriage partner has the right to physically or mentally impose himself or herself upon his or her mate. Coercive elements in marriage, physical or otherwise, are explosive and ultimately destructive to the marriage as well as the family. These efforts to coerce or force our spouses, used to whatever degree or in whatever manner, bring about that misery in which Satan finds so much satisfaction.

The Lord says that priesthood power is inseparably connected to heaven only upon the principles of righteousness, which include kindness, long-suffering, patience, and so forth. (See D&C 121:41-42.) If we do not incorporate these character traits into our marriage and family relationships, we will leave ourselves exposed to the powers of Satan, and no matter how we excuse ourselves, we are not exercising righteous dominion. And if our exercising of power over others is not righteous, then we too will find ourselves upon that plain of misery so graphically described by Dr. Ritchie.

As a final commentary regarding the satanic destruction from spouse and child abuse, consider carefully the words of President Gordon B. Hinckley as he spoke in the priesthood session of the 155th semi-annual conference of The Church of Jesus Christ of Latter-day Saints, on October 5, 1985: "No man who has been ordained to the priesthood of God can with impunity indulge in either spouse or child abuse. Such activity becomes an immediate repudiation of his right to hold and exercise the priesthood and to retain membership in the Church."

Can there be any question that the consuming splashes and engulfing ripples of this monstrous sin, if not fully repented of and resolved, will bring eternal damnation to the precipitator and lifelong suffering to the innocent victim?

If you have been involved in any way with this cancerous evil, please have the courage to share your experience with the appropriate priesthood authorities. Such courage will not only pave the way for relief to the victim, but it will also open the doors so that the perpetrator can approach the Savior for His divine forgiveness. Nothing you do will ever be more kind than that.

Let us now leave this area and consider another common form of "tilting" that afflicts so many Latter-day Saints—the lack of personal integrity or honesty.

California had been good for us. I was secure in my teaching position, with no debts to speak of. We were comfortable in our small home and had many friends. Yet after eleven years in California, we came to Utah to begin a new and challenging job.

Once in Utah, we secured the loan for our new home, and the work began. Our contractor gave us a list of the various expenditures to be made and the amount we could spend to stay within the amount of our loan. To save money, we did as much work on the home as we could, and we shopped carefully, and yet we had a great deal of fun choosing the lights, carpets, and other furnishings for our dream home.

For us, this was a time of thanksgiving, and we thanked the Lord daily for the opportunity that had been given us.

Everything was on schedule, and all appeared to be going well. However, about a month before the house was to be completed, we became aware that some of the subcontractors had not been paid for their labors. There were work stoppages and calls from workers wanting to be paid.

We also began receiving phone calls from suppliers, and they too demanded payment. We were embarrassed and frustrated, to say the least. We met with our contractor, who told us not to worry, but that everything would be taken care of.

Finally, when the problems did not go away, we learned that there was nearly $25,000 in unpaid debts. The contractor, who was LDS, had taken draws on our loan but had not paid the debts for which the draws were intended.

We went to our bank to see how much money was left in our loan account. We were told that there was enough money for completing construction if the contractor would pay off the outstanding debts. The contractor assured us that he would do so, and so we continued the finishing work on our home. We also told the bank to stop all future draws from the contractor.

Finally the carpets were installed, the final inspection took place, and we moved into our home. The storm had been weathered, we were happy, and all seemed well. Then, three days later, we received a call from our bank telling us that there had been a computer error of nearly $20,000. Not only was there no money left, but the bank had disbursed $4,000 more than the loan amount.

A frantic call to the contractor brought reassurances, but in reality he was nearly bankrupt, and nothing was done. In fervent prayer we asked the Lord for guidance and for peace of mind. The answers always came, but not always in the ways we had hoped.

There was now $32,000 in unpaid bills, and we had no personal funds left with which to pay them. Then the doorbell rang, and we received a court summons. A lawsuit was being placed against us and the contractor. We nearly died. Then, within days, another summons came.

By this time, we were completely overwhelmed and in near panic. Our contractor said that his attorney would take care of the whole matter, but we could no longer believe his words. It was then that we went to our bishop. He demonstrated sincere interest and counseled us to obtain legal direction.

Even though we had a strong case for a lawsuit, we did not want to pursue that course of action. Rather than sue, we determined to simply give up our home.

At that time we learned that our contractor was under extreme duress from several other parties who were seeking redress through lawsuits. However, we felt that bitterness and hatred could be our reward if we allowed ourselves to follow the same path. Besides, our contractor seemed sorry for his mistakes, and the bank officer was equally sorry for the bank's error.

Our home was so much a part of us. We designed it, worked on it, and put so much of our emotional selves into it. It was spacious, and it was the perfect home and neighborhood in which to raise our large family. Still, hard as it was, we chose to forgive, to sell our home and use our equity to repay the contractor's debts and to start fresh in life.

For us, that decision enabled us to understand this admonition of Christ: "If after thine enemy has come upon thee the first time, he repent and come unto thee praying thy forgiveness, thou shalt forgive him, and shalt hold it no more as a testimony against thine enemy." (D&C 98:39; see also verse 23.)

As we read the papers, listen to the news on television and radio, serve in our ecclesiastical callings, and go from day to day in our business affairs, it is amazing how many Latter-day Saints are dishonest. Strangely, most do not think of themselves as dishonest, but in one way or another they excuse themselves or their behavior.

"It is just business," says one.

"I wouldn't want to hurt their feelings," declares another.

"They're not mature enough to deal with the truth," advises a third.

Why is it that so many of us struggle with dishonesty? Why is it that so many people become dishonest in their efforts to acquire wealth? Might it be that we equate wealth with success? And success with righteousness?

Consider this quotation:

Utah's large Mormon population has become a prime target for con artists and swindlers who annually gyp the state's residents out of hundreds of millions of dollars. . . . Federal prosecutors say the state has gained a national reputation as "test market for scams. If it works here, they take it on the road. . . ." It has happened time and time again. . . .—It's very easy for people to bridge the gap from unbelievability to believability if church affiliation is used. . . .

The investor lists were drawn up on genealogy sheets used by church members to trace their ancestry. . . . Mormon leaders denounced the scheme in a stinging editorial which asked, "Why do people take chances like this? Why do people gamble?" One answer: "Their greed gland gets stuck. . . . In this culture, financial success is often equated with righteousness." (Peter Gillins, *Sunday Star Bulletin and Advertiser*, Honolulu, January 10, 1982.)

It seems to us that "on tilt" men and women who carry out such schemes, who try to take advantage of others financially, are servants of Satan who have become carriers of misery and barriers to joy. In the same manner, might it also be possible that we who are looking for the quick or easy road to wealth might also fall into the same category? Noted Latter-day Saint scholar Hugh Nibley wrote:

Why should we labor this unpleasant point? Because the Book of Mormon labors it, for our special benefit. Wealth is a jealous master who will not be served half-heartedly and will suffer no rival—not even God. . . . "Ye *cannot* serve God and Mammon." (Matthew 6:24.) In return for unquestioning obedience wealth promises security, power, position, and honors, in fact anything in this world. Above all, the Nephites like the Romans saw in it a mark of superiority and would do anything to get hold of it, for to them "money answereth all things." (Ecclesiastes 10:19.) . . . "Ye do always remember your riches," cried Samuel [the Lamanite], ". . . unto great swelling, envyings, strifes, malice, persecutions and murders, and all manner of iniquities." (Helaman 13:22.) Along with this, of course, everyone dresses in the height of fashion, the main point being always that the proper clothes are expensive—the expression "costly apparel" occurs 14 times in the Book of Mormon. The more important wealth is, the less important it is how one gets it. (Hugh Nibley, *Since Cumorah* [Salt Lake City: Deseret Book, 1970], pp. 393-94.)

Thus so many of us excuse cheating and dishonesty, hardly realizing at all the great danger we put ourselves in. In 2 Nephi 9:34, the prophet Jacob declares: "Wo unto the liar, for he shall be thrust down to hell."

There are probably many ways to interpret this scripture, but one might be that he who is dishonest in any way (a liar before God) places himself under the power of Satan. And that action, because of the loss of the Spirit of the Lord, who cannot abide evil in the least degree, must surely take immediate effect.

Of course, no intelligent person would want to intentionally place himself under Satan's power and dominion. Yet as we dishonestly make our foolish ways through life, it happens, and the splashes and ripples affect us and the lives of those about us.

If we are in a position where we are involved in "on tilt" behavior and can change, or where we can observe it and do something about it, we would be remiss if we did not. It is far better, if we are able, to further the cause of joy than misery, even though this might involve what is commonly called "hard love." Consider this illustration:

When I was a small child, I learned a lesson that has never left me. Every year our stake held a fathers and sons outing on our stake property near Morgan, Utah. On one outing all of us kids (I was in the fourth grade) found an old truck sitting on the property. It looked like it had been sitting there forever, and we assumed that it was no good and didn't belong to anyone.

It was our chance to finally let out all our inhibitions. Taking no thought about any circumstances that might have caused the truck to be left there, we fulfilled our own desires: A group of

95

about fourteen of us demolished that truck as you have never seen anything demolished before. We took a pickax and had a contest to see who could put the deepest holes in the body. We also smashed out all the windows, filled the gas tank with rocks, and picked up the biggest boulders we could lift to see how far we could dent in the sides.

Well, it turned out that we had destroyed the truck of an old man who had got stuck and hadn't been able to get back and retrieve his vehicle.

The bishopric and stake presidency were pretty upset, and the next Sunday we all had a council with our parents and the bishopric. We were all to pay for the damage to the truck by buying a new one for the owner. That truck was the old man's only way to get around, and we had wiped it out.

So the fourteen of us set out to earn $2,000, which is an awful lot of money for a bunch of fourth graders. Still, we worked until we had earned every cent of that truck back. And in the process, I learned a very valuable lesson.

Do you suppose I now act hastily on my own desires? You bet I don't! I think twice and then I think again, doing my best to assess the needs of others before I ever do *anything* that might hurt them. That was hard work earning all that money, but it was also one of the best lessons I have ever been taught.

To this point we have dealt with individual situations and problems. Consider, if you will, the rippling effect of an entire ward that forgot to care.

I come from a very close and spiritual family, in which we always relied on the Lord to give us direction and purpose. We have always attempted to do our part in helping those around us, and until this summer we have been at least as equally cared for by them.

At the beginning of the summer, my mother went to Germany for a month to visit her family. Two days after her departure, my father was operated on because he tore some ligaments in his knee. Because my elder sister, Becky, works eight hours a day, I had to visit the hospital each day and care for our father. Every day for a week I would visit him and spend most of the day by his side to assist him with his needs.

Because the operation was not too serious, our mother stayed in Germany. After a week, we brought our father home, thinking all was well. I had called the Relief Society president the day of his operation, but as yet no one in the ward had so much as contacted us.

My father could not get out of bed at all because his legs could not support him. His right leg had been operated on, and he was not allowed to put any weight on it. His left leg was very weak because he had had polio at the age of sixteen, leaving this leg crippled. He was bedridden, which meant I had to care completely for his needs. I was happy to do this for him and was relieved that he was home from the hospital.

At least, for a moment he was home. Saturday evening, after eating, my father was overcome with a stomach disorder, causing him to burp uncontrollably. Little did we know that at that moment Dad was within an inch of losing his life.

These burps continued through the night and were accompanied by a sharp pain under his left rib cage. When I finally contacted his doctor the following morning, we were instructed to get him immediately to the hospital. Before leaving, however, Dad requested that his home teachers give

him a priesthood blessing. His doctor had told us
that he was in jeopardy of dying, and so I quickly
called the home teachers, who were just a few blocks
away. After an hour and a half, they arrived. The
blessing was given, and then we left immediately for
the hospital.

The doctors indicated that he had arrived not a
minute too soon, and it was determined that he had
a blood clot in his left lung. By that time, the blood
clot had passed through his heart, leaving irreparable
damage to the heart. We fasted as a family, but as
the days passed, his condition worsened.

Realizing from the doctors that Dad could very
easily die, I called the bishop, our home teachers,
the Relief Society president, and my Laurel advisor,
asking for help and for their faith and prayers. The
only person to respond, several days later, was the
bishop, who visited Dad at the hospital. He
promised help from the ward, but still no one came
or even expressed concern.

Finally, two weeks later, Dad was released from
the hospital and returned home to convalesce. He
had been informed that his position at work had
been filled, leaving him without a job and without a
future. Many times he told me that he wished he
would die, and that no one seemed concerned with
whether he lived or died.

I was finally able to reach Mother by phone, as
she had returned to her family following an extended
tour through Europe. She had imagined that Dad
was fully recovered, and she left immediately for
home after she learned of his condition.

It was a long week later, after Mother's return,
that the Relief Society president visited, bringing
dinner. She expressed her happiness that Dad was
getting better and offered her "too little, too late"
assistance.

Some time has passed since our emergency, and

with its passing I have resolved that never will I stand idly by while someone I know is in need. I realize that we are all busy, and yet having once had a critical need myself, I hope to always respond with help, rather than with an all-too-late excuse for helping, or with no help at all.

Let's now pursue another area of concern. There are times when people get carried away by having, as they suppose, authority over others. If that authority is exercised in unrighteousness in any manner, a great deal of pain and embarrassment results. The Lord tells us that we can recognize these people because their hearts are set upon worldly things, and they aspire to the honors of men. (See D&C 121:34-35.) In the following account, consider how many people are affected by one such individual.

A young man went on a mission. In his first area, he was blessed with much success and was instrumental in bringing many people into the Church. He was quickly promoted to senior companion, and then to district and zone leader.

Through each of these promotions, this missionary became increasingly arrogant and haughty. He thought that he was better than the other missionaries who served with him. He would play pranks and speak disparagingly of his fellow companions. In addition, he became very authoritarian and chastised the members in his area for not providing investigators for the missionaries to teach. At the same time, he started wearing fancier suits, buying clothing of colors not compatible with missionary attire.

Some of the mission rules this elder completely ignored. He played racquetball every day, and he generally considered himself above the rules of the common missionary.

Finally, listening to the promptings of the Spirit,

the mission president felt impressed to call this elder in for an interview. The mission president found not only the above problems but learned that the other missionaries in this elder's zone were also engaging in inappropriate daily athletic activities.

The mission president told this elder that when the Lord gave us agency, he also saw to it that we would reap the consequences of our actions. The prideful elder was transferred to the city of the mission home and made a junior companion, while one of his former junior companions was made his zone leader. Transfers had been made only the week before, and so this incident was brought to the attention of the entire mission.

This action was very humbling to the elder, and at first he was resentful. As time passed, however, he realized that he had been in the wrong, and for the first time in his life he grew humble and repentant. Even though this was a painful and embarrassing experience, this elder and the members of his former zone are all better people for having gone through it.

It is interesting to think of the many ways a person "on tilt" can be brought back into an upright position. However, almost always, as in the account above, this process seems to include the workings of the Holy Ghost and an appropriate ecclesiastical leader. Isn't it intriguing that the Lord has set up his kingdom to include leaders filled with authority and revelation for those in their charge, who can and do bring tilted Saints back into the fold. Let us conclude this chapter with two joyful examples of this Godly process.

I have always enjoyed working in the Mutual, even during my teenage years as a youth leader. During the year preceding my mission, I had the opportunity to work with our stake presidency on the stake youth council. Our stake president was very concerned with the growing number of inactive youth in our stake, and with how many of them were using drugs and alcohol. Now, you need to know that this stake president is not a man to just sit and talk about problems and to take no action. He suggested to our council that we begin a "one-on-one" program where each active youth would select an inactive member to fellowship and to attempt to become friends with.

The members of our council determined that if we didn't reach our friends soon they might never come back into the Church. As a result, we decided as a stake to hold a special all-day fast for them and conclude the fast that evening with a testimony meeting, to which we would bring as many of these young people as would attend.

I didn't think these inactive friends were even aware that we were fasting that day, but I kept hearing kids at school talking about how they couldn't eat lunch because of the fast and how they had invited a friend to the meeting that night. I was really taken aback by this participation, because I didn't think that many of these active youth cared about what we were doing.

As I look back, I think of that evening's meeting as one of the most spiritual I have ever attended. Youth who were inactive seemed to fill the back rows of the overflow area of the chapel, and as the meeting and testimonies became more and more spontaneous, these inactive kids started to become involved. Girls as well as boys stood up with tears streaming down their faces, bearing their testimonies and saying how they had finally found out what real friends were. All this came about because of a stake president who truly cared.

I fell in love with a man who had been excommunicated, and so I guess you could say I came into the Church through the back door. But like the back doors of most homes, they generally lead to the warmest part of the home. If you are welcomed at the back door, you are welcomed as family. And that is how we were accepted in our new ward. My husband and I had constant friendship through the entire experience of both his and my repentance.

As members of this chosen church, we have a great responsibility to love—unconditionally. For some, this can be as difficult as the entire process of repentance. When one feels unworthy of love, even the slightest outpouring of kindness can seem like a floodtide. And love can be shown in so many ways— having the Relief Society president recognize you and not keep introducing you as a visitor, or a home teacher's prayer for continued learning in the home, or a dedicated seventy who shares the gospel in a spirit of love and joy, or just a friendly smile and a hand of fellowship when you walk into the church, or friends who stand by you, knowing you've made a big mistake and still saying, "That's my friend."

The Church was new to me, though I had been watching general conference for years and gleaning as much as I could through that. As my husband and I studied, I matured my study of the gospel with books on repentance and forgiveness. *The Miracle of Forgiveness* was to be at our sides for four years, and we gained hope from passages that expressed God's ultimate love and willingness to forgive. What a welcome word that was in our vocabulary!

We needed God's love, and we felt it daily through our prayers. As difficult as the road to repentance ultimately turned out to be, we were always thankful that there was a way back.

Forgiving others seemed to be the easy part, forgiving oneself the real challenge. Many had been hurt and a family had been torn apart, and it was not easy to get past the horrible reality of that. Still, as we struggled with the laws and lessons of repentance, we grew in our understanding of the gospel and its importance to us. Nothing seems precious until it is lost or taken away, and so it was with the gospel.

As we started the long road back, we knew there would be depression and days of heartache. But still the goal was set and the blessing of having the companionship of the Holy Ghost was a worthy, achievable goal. Still, to attend church and be a nonmember was like going to a basketball game and not being able to cheer. Not being able to take the sacrament and missing the blessings of paying tithing were some of the biggest heartaches of all.

The gift of the Holy Ghost was what we needed to help bring solutions to our problems. And even though we knew we could not have that gift, our prayers each day were for the Holy Ghost's guidance and comfort. Our hearts ached for this, and so many of our prayers were answered. Truly God does not leave man alone in need.

When it was announced that my husband could be rebaptized, we both knew that the years of hungering for the constant presence of the Holy Ghost were worth it. We yearned to be examples of Christ, to become all that Heavenly Father desired of us from the beginning. We knew we were taking upon us a great responsibility by being baptized, but we felt ready to do so. We had been taught so well and loved so well that we were anxious to give to others what had been given to us.

"Ye shall weep and lament and ye shall be sorrowful, but your sorrow shall be turned into joy." This Bible passage was brought to life on the day of our joint baptism. The back door of the home was wide open that day, and friends and family all welcomed us and shared in our joy. Spiritual joy is a day of sunshine that never ends, and that day at least three people basked in the sunshine that had the power to heal hardness of heart and deep, deep hurt and pain.

The seven responsibilities and obligations of baptism meant a great deal to my husband, who was being rebaptized, and to myself, who was being baptized for the first time. "Giving" became the buzzword in our lives, and we just couldn't wait to share what our Church leaders and others had given us.

If you will lean on the wondrous powers of Heavenly Father and his divine Son, blessings can be yours today. Never give up on the Lord, for he never gives up on you. Love unconditionally, study with great intensity, endure willingly, and pray as Jesus did in the Garden of Gethsemane, earnestly, sincerely, with real intent, and with all the energy and strength of your soul.

Do all that, and surely you will be cleansed as we were. Then you can look forward with joy and confidence, as do we, to meeting Heavenly Father.

CHAPTER FIVE

PATIENCE—GRATITUDE IN ADVERSITY

Throughout this book we have considered the two philosophies and hopes that exist regarding God's children. The Lord's philosophy and hope is that we will all have joy. Satan's philosophy and hope is that we will all become miserable—even as he is. Such being the case, we become disciples of either God or Satan, depending upon which of these philosophies and hopes we promulgate to our fellowman.

As a side note, some time ago Brenton attended the mission farewell of one of his former seminary officers, Margaret Benson, granddaughter of President Ezra Taft Benson and Sister Flora Benson. This justifiably proud grandmother, Sister Benson, gave her testimony, and then in conclusion she admonished the congregation by saying "May the Lord bless you and the devil miss you!"

It is our goal to see that this does happen in our lives, and we pass along her plea to you.

Few people wish to be disciples of Lucifer—those whom the scriptures call anti-Christs. Yet in so very many ways, because we seem undesirous or unable to change, we continue to inflict hurt and pain upon each other—either physically, mentally, emotionally, or spiritually; either intentionally or otherwise. And when we inflict pain or do nothing to divert it from those around us, we in effect become anti-Christs whether we choose to thus label ourselves or not.

How can we change? How can we assume Christ's discipleship and become barriers to misery and pain in others? What can we do to insure that we will respond to *all* situations in a caring or Christ-like way? How can we modify uncaring behavior that so frequently is based upon attitude-creating events that happened before we even have memories of those events?

The Lord has said: "He who receiveth all things with thankfulness shall be made glorious; and the things of this earth shall be added unto him, even an hundred fold, yea, more." (D&C 78:19.)

That is a powerful promise. Anyone who accepts *everything* that comes his way, including adversity, with sincere appreciation, will be given spiritual as well as temporal rewards.

Elder Neal A. Maxwell, in an address to the First Quorum of the Seventy, asks this question:

> Are we ready to follow the Lord into soul stretching experiences, to move forward . . . if it means having experiences that will teach us through suffering, just as Jesus learned through suffering—noted in that stunning scripture where Alma speaks of Jesus and his atonement and crucifixion: "And he shall go forth, suffering pains and afflictions and temptations of every kind; and this that the word might be fulfilled which saith he will take upon him the pains and the sicknesses of his people. And He will take upon him death, that he may loose the bands of death which bind his people; and he will take upon him their infirmities, that his bowels may be filled with mercy, according to the flesh, that he may know according to the flesh how to succor his people according to their infirmities." (Alma 7:11-12.)
>
> That you and I may need to suffer and undergo certain experiences . . . leaves us open to certain experiences we may not want, but which the Lord may bring upon us (for our own eternal good).

That is the key—to be able to accept the fact that God loves us, and to believe that in the eternal scheme of things, he will not allow a single bad (not the same as unpleasant) thing to happen to us. And that is his promise, so long as we are trying to live uprightly. For he has said: "Let your hearts be comforted; for all things shall work together for good to them that walk uprightly, and to the sanctification of the church." (D&C 100:15.)

Often we suffer for no apparent reason. That is, forces beyond our control converge to provide tidal waves of trials that we must weather. In the process, we invariably learn who we really are.

Because of earthquakes and volcanoes in Central and South America many thousands have lost their lives, loved ones, or property. The rest of the world offered their prayers and assistance in whatever way possible, but these quakes and eruptions have been some of the greatest tragedies in recent history. There was nothing anyone on earth could have done to prevent them. Yet still the disasters are there and must be coped with.

Consider the following true story that reflects the kinds of personal volcanoes and earthquakes we frequently seem to inherit from our mortal experience.

Bountiful, Utah *Clipper News*—"It takes a lot of willpower and persistence to succeed. But with them, almost anything can be accomplished—despite being paralyzed from the neck down."

Thus begins an article about a small giant named Lynn Crosbie Olsen. Lynn, at age seven, was struck by a car, leaving him paralyzed and almost lifeless. Within seconds after the mishap, a Layton fire truck passed the scene, and the firemen rushed to the little boy's side. He was not breathing. He had a broken neck, a broken back, and a crushed pelvis, and his leg was broken in two places.

For three days, young Lynn lay in a coma while his parents kept a prayerful vigil at his side. At last, against all medical odds, Lynn regained consciousness. His spinal cord was severed at the base of his neck, and though he was completely paralyzed, it was immediately apparent that his brain was exceptionally keen.

Months have passed since the accident. Lynn's life has been forever changed, but it certainly has not been diminished. He now has a private tutor and does his schoolwork at the same pace as before the accident. He even drives his hospital wheelchair—going forward, backing up, and turning,—all by blowing into a tube. A computer is presently being designed that will record messages from Lynn, change the television station, turn on the lights, and so on.

It became a creative effort for Lynn to be baptized when he reached the age of eight. He was determined, though, and approval was given to use the University of Utah rehabilitation swimming pool. Then, with a lifesaving air bag attached, five men slowly dunked Lynn's body into the water. He came up smiling, and with expressions that clearly stated that he wanted to do it again.

Since turning eight, Lynn has earned his Bobcat and Wolf Cub Scout awards. Even though he is fed intravaneously and is unable to speak, Lynn communicates his feelings and his spirit to his family as well as to all those who have stepped forward to assist him.

As we consider the long-range effects of Lynn's accident, we become aware that many times our unrequested trials will last throughout mortality. These trials have nothing to do with our level of righteousness—they are just there. Still, we will be rewarded by God according to how we deal with them—becoming, in the process, disciples of Christ, who himself suffered with such total dignity.

We have a dear friend, Clive Andersen, who, with his

wife, Mary Lou, has taught us a great deal about this concept. They have several children. One of them, a son, was
born with 15 percent brain capacity. He cannot talk, eat,
walk, or care for his personal needs, and he may not even
recognize his parents and family. Still, because they understand the principle of Christ-like love in adversity, Clive
and Mary Lou have cared for their son without complaint
and with unqualified love for the past nineteen years.

Can such a couple help but become Christ-like through
their loving service? And will not the ripples of their selfless
love go out to acquaintances and posterity for generations to
come? Truly Clive and Mary Lou are *becoming.*

And now another story, this time from a young man who
writes about his younger brother, and who is having a lifelong experience in becoming a disciple of Christ.

His name is Scott. He is four years old, but unlike
many others of his age, Scott is different—he has
Down's syndrome. Scott has been a special influence
in many facets of my life. However, it was
specifically through his birth that our family grew
closer together in love, and I learned how much our
neighbors, friends, and relatives really cared.

Our family was quite anxious for the birth of our
next family member. Though my mother had been
somewhat ill during this pregnancy, none of us gave
much thought to the baby's health as it grew within
her body.

Finally the day came. My parents left for the
hospital, and for some time we children all waited
expectantly. It was late afternoon when Dad finally
returned home. As he walked through the door, I
could sense an air of sadness. I didn't know what to
expect, but I braced myself.

"Your new brother is very special," is the first
thing that Dad said. "He is mentally retarded."

It wasn't until Dad began to weep that I
understood the seriousness of the situation. "Now,"

he went on, "I want you to think this over very carefully. The doctor recommended immediate commitment to an institution. Mother and I both feel that this ought to be a family decision. If we decide to keep him, it's going to take lots of time, patience, and especially love. Will you accept this baby into our family?"

There was really never any hesitation in my mind. I realized how much I loved and cared for each member of my family, and without even seeing my new little brother, I knew that I loved and wanted him also.

We all knelt down in prayer and asked the Lord for his guidance. When we finished praying, we all looked at each other and unanimously knew the answer to our question.

That day our family accepted a new little brother, and through our love for him we have likewise learned to more completely love each other. In addition, the response shown by others has been unbelievable. The persistent ringing of the telephone often interrupted thoughtful neighbors at the door, as many tried to help us adjust to our new situation. Though it wasn't a sad or tragic experience, many who did not fully understand still expressed their care by trying to console us. It truly seemed that everyone was willing to help and everyone cared.

It has been four years since Scott became my brother, and I have never regretted accepting him into our family. I know that Scott is a blessing sent from God to help all of us grow. It's just an honor to think that the Lord loved my family enough to give us this great experience.

Another earthquake account—this time in the life of a father and husband. Yet truly this earthquake created an opportunity for much loving service from a daughter.

I have a friend named Diane. She loves her father, but I think it is more than that which impels her to give him so much. Diane is married and has one daughter. Each day she takes her daughter and goes to her parents' house to care for her father while her mother is at work.

I don't know much about Diane's father except that he is disabled but does not actually need twenty-four-hour care. Diane just goes to keep him company and to help him keep his spirits up. She says she thinks it would be hard for a man who has supported a family all of his life to see that task taken over by his wife, and then to sit home alone each day waiting for her to return from work. Diane spends her time with him to ease the pain of that trial.

As a young mother, Diane feels that she also has a life of her own to live. Still, she gives of herself to her father each and every day, and is an example of service I hope always to follow.

All of us have constant opportunities to send out appropriate ripples, affecting for good those around us. But few have the opportunity to influence others that is given to parents. In the following account from a daughter, we learn of a father who is teaching in the best manner possible how to become a disciple of Christ.

Last summer Brother Jacobs, an elderly temple worker, had a stroke and was taken to the hospital. My father was his home teacher, and visited him often. He also checked in on Sister Jacobs weekly.

After several weeks, Brother Jacobs was progressing nicely and seemed to be doing quite well. Then suddenly, without warning, he had another stroke that left him paralyzed.

Dad continued to visit Brother Jacobs, but the elderly man's condition grew steadily worse. Soon he had lost his memory and had no idea who was in the room with him. Still my dad continued his visits.

Gangrene now set in, and Brother Jacobs lost his leg. Then he began to lose his sight. There he lay in his hospital bed, slowly dying. The orderlies did not enjoy feeding or shaving him, for he was not a pleasant sight. So, before Sister Jacobs would come to visit her beloved husband, my father would go into the room and shave the old man's face.

For weeks this routine continued; the weeks became months, and still the old man clung to life. He could recognize no one, he had no idea what was going on around him, and yet he continued to live.

One Sunday after church, my father asked the family if we could wait while he stopped at the hospital on our way home. It was a hot and muggy day, but we agreed if Dad promised not to take too long.

Later, on our way home, I asked Dad if Brother Jacobs had recognized him.

"No," was his reply, "I don't think so."

Throughout the next week I wondered why Dad would continue to visit a person who did not even know he was there. What difference could Dad's visits possibly make?

One week later Brother Jacobs passed away, and my father was given the task of dressing his body for the funeral. At the viewing, Brother Jacobs looked so peaceful. As my father stood beside the casket of the man he had been assigned to love, I finally realized that his caring was true charity, the pure love of Christ.

We would like to share a different type of story now, this time of a family we know who quietly share their message of charity, even though the sorrow is still there and the outcome is still in doubt.

When I was three years old, Mom and Dad met a little boy. His mother had abused him, and he had been taken away from her. Since that time, he had been in several foster homes, and more than anything else, he wanted a real mother and father.

Our family accepted this boy for a trial period and gradually learned about him. He had many emotional problems, had had cerebral palsy, and was not very coordinated. He had also been born without a complete abdominal wall, and he had many other problems.

Our brother was six when we brought him into our home and into our hearts. He slept in a fetal position and would lie down and rock back and forth humming. Sometimes he would throw violent temper tantrums. In addition, he was not yet able to care for himself.

Mom and Dad put him in a private kindergarten, only to be told that he was mentally retarded and not acceptable. They fought this information, but still our brother was removed from the school.

At this time we held a family council, and all of us decided to adopt him. Even though at the time we knew a great deal about what to expect, it took years to learn what a burden we had taken upon ourselves. Mom spent countless hours helping him with his studies, more time probably than she gave all of the rest of us put together.

Our brother loved to participate in church, but when he turned fifteen, he began to change. Suddenly he was doing all of the things he had been taught not to do. He took checks from Mom and Dad and forged them, and he was constantly in trouble at school. Finally, Social Services told Mom and Dad that the agency could not assist them further. He would have to be placed in a special school.

Mom and Dad had two daughters in college, and the recommended school was terribly expensive. To fund my brother's expenses, Mom and Dad sold their home, swimming pool and all, and we moved to a trailer park near our brother's school. It wasn't easy, but we did it because our brother needed the help, and he needed our love and closeness as well.

I wish this account had a happy ending, but it doesn't. My brother has been out of school now for two years. He came home resenting Mom and Dad for having put him there, and he still does everything he can to let them know of his resentment. He rarely works, is not active in the Church, and, because of his attitude, it is difficult for him to be happy or successful. We often wonder if all of the sacrificing was worth it, but Mom and Dad tell us repeatedly that it was, and that one day our brother will become a happy person. I hope so.

And now, two final experiences that show the diligent efforts of ordinary people to become Christ-like. The first deals with members of Brenton's ward when he served as bishop. Even though these folks will fuss at Brent for revealing their names, he feels the risk is worth it—simply because of their unique and unified greatness, which reflects true discipleship in the face of adversity.

Earl and Gina Vancil are remarkable! Even though they would not have requested the adversity they have fallen heir to, they have accepted it with miraculous and unobtrusive gratitude.

Several years ago Earl shot off his leg in a hunting accident. In addition, Earl has contracted lymphoma, has Baker's cyst in his right knee, has had three operations for blockages in his prostate, has been hospitalized three times for kidney stones, has been bitten by a copperhead snake (resulting in five days of intensive care in the hospital), has diabetes type II (and so is insulin dependent), and has been hospitalized three times for pneumonia. Also, he broke three ribs falling in the bathtub following his leg amputation, crushed his left hand in machinery at his work, contracted sclerosis of the liver due to having chronic hepatitis, has had kidney failure and subsequent removal of a kidney, and has been hospitalized six times for failure of his second kidney. He developed osteomyelitis in his sternum and rib cage following open-heart surgery, was hospitalized three times with thrombophlebitis, has severe progressive atherosclerotic heart disease, and has been hospitalized five times for impaired liver function.

As if these problems were not enough for Earl and Gina, Earl has developed severe allergies to pain-killing medicines, has had several skin cancers removed, has a growth on his larynx that will soon need surgery, has been hospitalized for knee cartilage removal following an automobile accident, has had two operations for hemorrhoids, was hospitalized for a fistula repair, has had a tumor removed from his left eye, has had a peptic ulcer removed, has had two hernia operations, has had an appendectomy, has had a nasal septal reconstruction due to an old football injury, has had two operations on his gall bladder—the later one to remove it—and has had a metatarsal tunnel syndrome operation.

In addition, if you can believe it, Earl has had a laminectomy and fusion of four vertebrae in his spine, has had a rotary cuff tear (and thus a subsequent right shoulder repair operation), and has had six surgical procedures for arteriograms, has had triple bypass open-heart surgery, and then has subsequently had a second and third open-heart surgery, to further allow his heart to keep ticking. On top of all this, he has contracted meningitis.

Beyond that, Earl has been hospitalized

approximately thirty-five times in addition to the above specific incidents—for various diagnostic and miscellaneous reasons.

As a stake, we just released Earl from an eighteen-month stake mission, and during his weeks out of the hospital he taught and baptized twelve people. In addition, this summer Earl was given an acre of land to work. Because of who this man is, he donated the harvest to others in need after he had personally planted, nurtured, and then reaped the following:

Eight bushels of green beans
Over 600 pounds of red potatoes
Over 300 pounds of squash
Over sixty bushels of tomatoes— from 425 plants
One-half acre of sweet corn
Over eight bushels of cucumbers
One-half pickup load of cantaloupes
Ten bushels of apples
Ten bushels of peaches
In addition, Earl bottled over 350 jars of pickles, peaches, cherries, tomatoes, tomato sauce, jellies, and jams—and freely gave them to those in need. *And all of this Earl did between hospital visits, and with a worn-out heart and a wooden leg!*

Whew! If you're like us, just reading about this true disciple has worn you out. If it has, set down the book, go outside and take a deep breath—and recall that we do not need to feel intimidated by this example, only inspired. Remember, God's greatest act of creativity is our own individuality. He created our differences; let us not berate ourselves for them.

The following is the story of an immigrant couple from Hungary who live in Novato, California, where their stake president, Len Ellis (also the dearest of friends) gives the following account:

Jabba Ju Kash and his wife, Valeria, left Hungary three years ago to settle in America. They had to leave behind their eleven-year-old daughter, but because of their desire for freedom, they felt the sacrifice was worth the separation. Jabba and Valeria touched American soil, both unable to speak a word of English, and neither able to drive a car or get a job.

One can imagine this couple's joy as the LDS missionaries found and taught them, and then as they embraced the gospel and were baptized just eighteen months ago.

Not long after Jabba and Valeria were baptized, a cultural difference caused Valeria embarrassment. As a result, she withdrew from activity in the Church, developing bitterness and resentment for the way she had been treated. At that time she put her crucifix back around her neck and announced that she would have nothing more to do with the Mormons.

I learned of this unfortunate circumstance, and so after sharing bits and pieces with my wife, Elaine, she decided that she would visit Valeria and offer her friendship. This Elaine did, baking a cake first, and then driving into the low-income housing area where the Kash family lived. This couple had no phone, and so Elaine was forced to knock on their front door unannounced—cake in hand. Valeria came to the door. Elaine introduced herself and then gave the cake to this beautiful woman. Sensing some kind of entrapment, Valeria exclaimed, "I'm Catholic—no cake, no cake."

Well, Elaine finally convinced Valeria that giving the cake was done simply in friendship, and then she left the front porch. Not long after that, and wanting to follow up with her feelings for this special and lonely immigrant, Elaine wrote her a note. In it she reintroduced herself and indicated that she wanted only to be a friend, and that she would visit Valeria again soon.

Not long after that, Elaine went back to the Kash home and was invited in by Valeria. My wife had previously asked me what I thought Valeria needed, and I said that I thought she might miss shopping at open markets such as she was accustomed to doing in her homeland. And so, Elaine went to visit Valeria every Thursday from that time forth and would take her to the open markets in the area.

Meanwhile, Valeria and Jabba's daughter, who was now fourteen, arrived from Hungary, and the family was at last together, adjusting to their new way of life. During this time Valeria also gave birth to a new American, a beautiful dark-haired son.

As one might guess, Elaine became good friends with Valeria and soon enrolled her in English classes. In addition, Elaine was able to gain Valeria's trust, and soon this sister was attending Relief Society with her. At this time the priesthood brethren again became involved with the Kash family and gave them support during the baby's birth, and much happiness was becoming evident in their home. Elaine hosted a baby shower for Valeria just after the birth, and Kash's home teacher, who is a convert from Peru, became a close friend of the family as well.

In all, this has been a very special experience for our family, for our ward, and for the people in our stake. Through Elaine's example, we have been able to see the fruits of reaching out, caring through a unique kind of adversity, and then becoming eternal friends to a family who, in spite of all obstacles, have gained freedom and true happiness through the gospel of Jesus Christ.

Earthquakes come and volcanoes erupt, and often we are given no idea if or when they will end. Whether we are victims ourselves, or whether we simply live in the area of conflict and so are able to influence those who suffer directly, we find that these are the moments when true discipleship emerges—if we respond as our Master would have us, with faith, gratitude, and love.

CHAPTER SIX

GODLINESS—DIRECTIONS FROM THE SPIRIT

To this point, we have discussed man-made ripples—acts, events, and influences that affect our personal righteousness, our ability to love and serve others, and our attitudes about life and God, our Father, who gave it to us. Now let us consider the ripples sent out from the Lord, celestial and spiritual impulses designed to help us become disciples, achieve happiness, and ultimately reach Godliness.

First, though, understand that we venture into this area with a certain amount of hesitation, for we know that our comprehension of this subject is very limited. Yet even that limited understanding of spirituality has repeatedly influenced our lives. The impressions of the Spirit of God have brought us further knowledge, truth, and motivation to change than could have come in any other way. We have learned truths about ourselves, reduced unnecessary dependence upon others, and experienced joy and peace that cannot be described. All of this has come about because of communications from the Spirit of God, which we so imperfectly receive and yet which we wish to discuss.

These impulses of the Spirit, according to the scriptures and the prophets, come with great regularity and with great universality. We communicate with God through prayer, and he communicates with us through inspiration, which occurs in a wide variety of ways: dreams, visions, promptings, impressions, parental counsel, direct revelation, and so on. However, not always are these varied celestial directions or impressions recognized, and in fact often they are not even wanted at all. Consider this example from a friend.

> As a young seminary teacher, I shared many spiritual experiences with my students. I thought I was helping them to understand the workings of the Spirit, but soon word began to filter back that these students, as well as many of their parents, did not believe me. Because they had not had similar experiences, they were certain I was either lying or exaggerating in order to maintain attention in my classes.
>
> After two years of dealing with this situation, I finally determined, after counseling with Dad, to keep my personal spiritual experiences to myself, to share them with no one but my immediate family unless I was certain I had been prompted otherwise.
>
> Years later, one of these students, now a returned missionary, approached me and apologized for his unbelief. "I wish I had trusted you," he said. "I have felt the workings of the Spirit in so many ways since my seminary days, and they would have been so much easier to understand if I had only believed they could really happen when you tried to teach me about them."

This young man learned well from the things he experienced on his mission and in his life. His seminary teacher learned that sacred experiences ought not to be indiscriminately shared. Truly they exist, but each individual has the responsibility to maintain his confidence with the Lord, sharing those experiences only when the Spirit directs.

Still, because we fear or do not understand, many of us

deny the workings of the Spirit altogether and so deny ourselves eternal blessings. The great prophets Mormon and his
son Moroni say it this way:

> Wo unto him that shall deny the revelations of the
> Lord, and that shall say the Lord no longer worketh by rev-
> elation, or by prophecy, or by gifts, or by tongues, or by heal-
> ings, or by the power of the Holy Ghost! (3 Nephi 29:6.)

> I exhort you, my brethren, that ye deny not the gifts of
> God, for they are many; and they come from the same God.
> And there are different ways that these gifts are adminis-
> tered; but it is the same God who worketh all in all; and they
> are given by the manifestations of the Spirit of God unto
> men, to profit them. (Moroni 10:8.)

Joseph Smith, the first prophet of our dispensation, in
sharing his profound experience in the Sacred Grove, en-
countered almost universal opposition and disbelief. He described his response to this disbelief in the following manner:

> It was . . . a fact that I had beheld a vision. I have
> thought since, that I felt much like Paul, when he made his
> defense before King Agrippa, and related the account of the
> vision he had when he saw a light, and heard a voice; but
> still there were but few who believed him; some said he was
> dishonest, others said he was mad; and he was ridiculed and
> reviled. But this did not destroy the reality of his vision. He
> had seen a vision, he knew he had, and all the persecution
> under heaven could not make it otherwise; and though they
> should persecute him unto death, yet he knew, and would
> know to his latest breath, that he had both seen a light and
> heard a voice speaking unto him, and all the world could not
> make him think or believe otherwise.
> So it was with me. I had actually seen a light, and in the
> midst of that light I saw two Personages, and they did in re-
> ality speak to me. (Joseph Smith—History 1:24-25.)

A good friend of ours, working diligently on her genealogy, became well acquainted with her great-grandmother,
who had passed on. This relationship with someone on the

other side of the veil was very sacred to her, and she longed with all her heart to share it with her loved ones. Finally she shared it with her parents and was almost cut off from her extended family because her parents could not accept what she had told them.

The point we are making is that spiritual manifestations not only do, but *should,* occur in our lives. We are not saying that these sacred experiences be shared indisciminitely with others, for they should not. Nevertheless, all of us have the obligation to ourselves and to our families to become spiritually minded so that the Lord can direct us back into his presence.

So, are we spiritual in nature? Do we believe that the power of God gives us inspiration, revelation, and guidance? Do we accept the reality of spiritual forces we cannot see? Are we conscious of the love and concern untold generations of ancestors have for us? Can we believe that God desires to give us both the strength and wisdom required to become disciples of his Son Jesus Christ, and that he will do so through the promptings of his Spirit?

The following test of spirituality, compiled by our dear friend Bernell L. Christensen, might help you answer these questions.

Test of Spirituality

1. *Prayer.* Have you ever had a specific prayer answered (where you were lifted beyond yourself, gained a previously unknown understanding or concept, had a warm feeling)?

2. *Scriptures.* Have you had an answer to a question come from the scriptures? (Or understand by the Spirit the meaning of a scripture, had the scriptures opened to your understanding, cried while reading, or known that what you are reading is true?)

3. *Spiritual prompting.* Have you ever had a spiritual prompting or feeling (the still, small voice; a feeling to do or not do something)?

4. *Parents*. When your parents were praying, did you feel that the prayer would be answered? Have you had a spiritual feeling in your home?

5. *Conscience*. Have you ever felt that something you did or were going to do was not right? Have you felt sorry, or scared, or hurt about something?

6. *Music*. Have you had a spiritual feeling or good feeling, or felt warm or felt like crying during a hymn?

7. *Love*. Have you felt a strong spiritual love or concern toward someone or from someone? (This could be toward parents, friends, teachers, or priesthood leaders. It might not include a girl or boy friend, but it could.)

8. *Sacrament*. During the administration of the sacrament, have you felt the words of the prayers in your soul, or felt your soul soothed with forgiveness or filled with the Spirit? Have you felt the love of the Savior?

9. *Testimony*. During a testimony meeting, have you felt that you should bear your testimony? Or, have you felt that the testimony of another was true?

10. *Pure intelligence*. Have you been inspired with new knowledge, or gained a clear understanding you didn't have before, or knew you were going to be asked to pray?

11. *Temple*. While in the temple, have you felt a sense of sacredness? Did you seek for and gain a greater understanding of the sacred ordinances therein?

12. *Patriarchal blessing*. While receiving or later reading your patriarchal blessing, have you felt the power of the patriarch, felt the thinness of the veil to the Spirit world, or gained an understanding of who you really are and what you are supposed to do?

13. *Ordination*. When being set apart or ordained, or while performing these ordinances for others, have you felt power, spiritual fire, or virtue pass from one to another?

14. *Priesthood blessing*. When you either received or gave a priesthood blessing, have you felt the power and inspiration of the Lord, or felt the virtue or the power of the Spirit?

15. *Beyond natural ability.* Have you given a talk or taught beyond your own ability?

16. *Spiritual gifts.* Do you have or have you experienced any of the gifts of the Spirit, such as visions, revelations, healings, or testimony?

17. *Daily spiritual experiences.* Do you have daily spiritual experiences?

We hope that answering these questions has given you cause for inner confidence, and that you have felt the influence of the Holy Ghost in one or more of the areas mentioned. If you are like us, these moments of reflection have also motivated you to spiritually move yourself beyond the experiences you have already had.

To the Lord, all things are spiritual. Once we accept that and learn to be in tune with his Spirit in these areas, we will begin having and learning from spiritual experiences. Consider this account:

> Several years ago, my wife was taken from mortality in an automobile accident. Our children were young and our family needs were great, and her death seemed so untimely to me. Yet my children and I weathered the storm. I realized that the Lord still loved me and was blessing me continually, and within three years I was married again—once more for eternity, and once more to a beautiful and spiritual companion.
>
> Over the course of the next several years, our family experienced the normal ups and downs of two families trying to weld themselves into one. There were many days when I wished I had never attempted it, and I know my wife felt the same. She had the worst of it, too, because the children made her the brunt of their own loneliness and frustrations.
>
> Amazingly, when these moments reached crescendos of crisis, both my wife and I, and quite

often one or more of our children, would sense the presence of my deceased wife. She brought a spirit of peace with her that always helped to settle our family differences.

Years passed, and my first wife's involvement with our mortal family grew to be accepted by all of us. We did not talk of it except occasionally with each other, but many experiences too sacred to be shared occurred, and we all grew in faith and an awareness of the close proximity of those who dwell in the world of spirits.

Then my second wife and I were called to serve the Lord as proselyting missionaries. We were thrilled, and we eagerly awaited the day we would be set apart for that work. When finally the stake president placed his hands upon my head, he gave me a most unusual and informative blessing.

"I bless you," he said, "that, with your *wives*, you will serve successfully and with great joy in your field of labor."

Our mission is now concluded, and words could never adequately express the joy that both of my wives and I found in that service. And I testify sincerely, as does my earthly sweetheart, that my deceased wife was literally a companion to us throughout our many months of service, in direct fulfillment of our stake president's blessing.

Can you imagine how this man's family has been affected spiritually by his and his mortal wife's candid acceptance of and interaction with his first wife? How can children reared in such a trusting and faith-filled environment be anything but spiritually minded? This becomes, for them all, a pure and true rippling of righteousness that will surely last for generations to come.

President David O. McKay said, "Spirituality is best expressed in doing, not in dreaming." (*Treasures of Life*, [Salt Lake City: Deseret Book, 1962], p. 263.)

In the second chapter of Ether we are told that, for one reason or another, the prophet known as the Brother of Jared had not called upon the name of the Lord for four long years. The Lord then came in a cloud and chastened him for three hours, after which he told the Brother of Jared to build barges for the Jaredites' upcoming journey.

At last obedient, the Brother of Jared completed the barges and then went once more before the Lord. "Two problems exist," he said, "First, we cannot see. And second, we cannot breathe."

Instantly the Lord directed the Brother of Jared to make holes in the tops and bottoms of the barges so that air could come in. The Brother of Jared did so, and thus the second problem was solved.

"Now what about light?" he asked next. And here we begin a most remarkable lesson. That time the Lord did not give the Brother of Jared any solutions. Instead, he asked simply, "What would you have me do?"

Thinking deeply, the Brother of Jared at last came up with an unusual solution (since windows and fire had already been eliminated by the Lord). Going to work, he melted out of the mountain sixteen small stones. Now he could easily have picked up sixteen stones from the bed of a stream that probably ran nearby, or he could have shattered some boulder into sixteen pieces and used them. We feel it is significant that he didn't. Instead he went to work and, to the best of his ability, melted out the finest rocks he could fashion, smooth and clear like glass.

Climbing to the top of the mount (going to a holy place) and coming once again before the Lord, the Brother of Jared then admitted both his efforts and his mortal limitations.

"Lord," he said, "I have done my best, but these things are still rocks, and I haven't any power to change that. You, on the other hand, have *all* power, so just touch them with your finger, and they will be turned into lights. Then we can travel."

Following that touching testimony and expression of absolute faith, the Lord apparently had no choice but to comply.

127

He touched the stones, and they became lights. The Brother of Jared saw the Lord's finger and fell back in fear. Questions were asked and answered, and at last the Lord revealed his entire person to the Brother of Jared, who, because of his exceeding faith, could not be kept without the veil.

But the point we would like to make is this. The Brother of Jared obtained answers to his prayers only after taking action himself. Further, he taught us that each of us must obtain answers to our prayers in the same manner.

First we go to the Lord or one of his earthly representatives with our problem. Then we are obedient to what we are told to do. Third, we creatively try to do even better than before with what we have been asked to do, or we creatively come up with what we consider the best possible solution to our problem. Finally, in pure faith, we go before the Lord again and ask him to make the solution his instead of just our own. If he does, we will know it by the burning we feel. If he does not, we will also know it by the stupor of thought that comes. Either way, we have obtained the answer we so diligently sought.

Thus if we are praying for the ability to forgive or to make our love more manifest or more pure, that will come about partly because our previous efforts at loving have already been manifested before the Lord.

President Spencer W. Kimball stressed through his entire tenure as Prophet the necessity of rendering quiet Christian service in addition to the other duties to which we have been called. It seems to us that by quietly reaching out, going beyond ourselves in helping others, our spirits become disciplined to the point where they are more susceptible to the promptings of God, and we are no longer kept in darkness outside his presence.

We have a friend whose secretary is a very special person. This secretary is divorced, and has several children she has reared by herself, and yet she has remained independent of outside assistance.

As time passed, our friend noticed that this woman's car was in great need of a new paint job. He knew she would never agree to let him help her, and so he asked if he could borrow her car over the weekend. In her usual compassionate way, this woman immediately agreed.

Our friend then took the car and had it sanded and painted. Then he handed her the keys the following Monday morning. As she had arrived earlier from the bus stop, this woman had not even recognized her own newly painted car in the parking lot. And so, feeling thankful that she had been able to help her supervisor, she accepted her keys from him and continued her morning tasks.

It was not until lunchtime that our friend looked up from his desk to see his secretary, her eyes filled with tears, stammering out her surprise and gratitude. She had gone to the parking lot, had seen her car, and had felt the joy of receiving in a righteous way. Both our friend and his secretary learned a great deal about both sides of giving that day, but it was our friend, we think, who gained the most. By doing, he *became,* and though he has not spoken of it to us, his wife has informed us that the impressions of the Spirit have given him what he calls an indescribable peace, just because of that one act of unsolicited kindness.

And now, as we conclude our consideration of direct communication to and from the Lord, let us share with you one last spiritual experience, a rather unusual one, that we have taken from the journals of a woman who has surely become a disciple of the Lord Jesus Christ.

Susan's Journal: November 15, 1979

Tonight I write an account of events that have transpired during the last two weeks. About two weeks ago I dreamed I was no longer on the earth. My physical body was lying in a casket. I could see myself clearly, and yet I was not at all frightened. The next night I felt the presence of a good spirit, a choice spirit, someone from the other side of the veil. When I finally went to sleep that night, I was not sure I would awaken, except in the world of spirits. Still, my thoughts were that in many ways I was not ready to die. I especially knew I had to complete my grandparents' genealogical and temple work.

I discussed the events of these nights with my friend Linda. I told her that I felt from those experiences that my time on earth was short—days, weeks, I didn't know.

The next two nights were similar. The being from the spirit world was still around. Mom and Dad and others who may one day read these words, please understand that I know these experiences have been given me by Heavenly Father. Please heed my words. The time is short. It goes fast. Who knows how long we have here? My feelings have not changed in the two weeks since all this happened. I still feel my time is short—shorter than I sometimes wish. I also feel that I will die by injuries to my head. That part frightens me a little, but I hope when it happens, it will happen quickly.

Mom and Dad, I know I will see you again, so that means I'll see Thanksgiving in Great Falls. Beyond that, and into December and January, I cannot see myself on this earth. I have attempted to set goals, but to no avail.

Mom and Dad, when you read this, please know that I love our Heavenly Father and that my testimony of Christ and his Church is strong. I want you to be with me someday, so please heed my words and make the gospel important in your lives.

I feel like January is my checking-in time, but my patriarchal blessing tells me that if my desires are righteous, Heavenly Father will grant them. I am pondering and studying to decide if I should petition him for more time here in mortality. I do not know if I will. Meanwhile my plan is to prepare for earth life as if I were going to be here for thirty years and live so that I could die tomorrow and be happy.

Susan did just as she promised. She set twelve long-range goals, including managing her time and marrying in the temple. She had already served a full-time mission and was at that time teaching elementary school several hundred miles from her home.

She continued to ponder her dreams and impressions; finally she decided, after receiving strong impressions from the Spirit, that she should tell no one other than her friend Linda of her feelings. She wanted to tell her parents, but they were inactive in the Church, and she felt that such a graphic pronouncement would do more harm than good. Thus she decided to shield them from what the Spirit had revealed to her.

Rather than tell them, she determined to record her feelings and her testimony in her journal, and then she began to pray constantly that the Lord would inspire her parents to read her words after she had gone.

Susan's Journal: November 17, 1979
My spirit friend hasn't been with me for two days. It has been a choice experience, but it isn't over. I feel that after Thanksgiving I will know what I'm doing. However, I will not be able to share that with anyone—not even you, Mom and Dad. My pending passing on is not scary. I've adjusted to it. If I die and you read this, please adjust to my death too. Life goes on for both of us. I'll be moving forward and you'll need to be moving forward, also.
Just a thought. In spite of what I've felt, I truly desire to choose a mate here on earth, to have a family, and to raise that family in righteousness.

In the days to come, Susan made a will in her journal and continued bearing testimony to her family of the truthfulness and importance of the gospel of Jesus Christ. Then, on November 24, she and Linda drove to the Cardston Temple in Alberta, Canada. She records:

We went the distance with little sleep. I slept for
half an hour, and Linda slept while I was inside the
temple. I took in one session, and my thoughts to
the Lord were centered around whether or not I
should live longer here in mortality. My attitude
changed there in the temple, and I realized that I
desired more time. I prayed for that, and the Lord
has given me three to five years extended time. I'll
use it well. I've made commitments I must keep.

As the weeks and months passed by, Susan continued to
encourage her family into church activity. Recording constantly in her journals, she spoke of her joy that some of her
family members were now attending church. She continued
to teach school, and more than anything else she worried
that she was not using her additional time wisely.

Twenty-four months and many spiritual experiences
later, all of which were faithfully recorded in her journals,
Susan was introduced to a young airman who was stationed
near her parents' home. They dated through the Christmas
season of 1981, they spent long hours discussing the gospel,
and in the spring of the following year the young man requested baptism into the Church.

By this time, Susan was deeply in love, and she was ec-
static when at last her boyfriend proposed marriage.

Susan's Journal: February 16, 1982
———— almost proposed to me today, but
wanted to wait until we were together in person.
Am I ready? I love him, he loves me. I must pray
about it, for my patriarchal blessing tells me I am to
marry an elder in Israel. Of course, now that he is
baptized, it won't be too long until he receives the
Melchizedek Priesthood. He will make a great
husband and father. I must sincerely pray about it.

Susan's Journal: February 21, 1982
Tonight at 10:00 P.M. ———— and I sat in the

car at Giant Springs, and he asked me to marry him.
Finally I said *yes*. I love him, Mom and Dad love
him, everyone in the family thinks he's great. I feel
on cloud nine tonight. I'm tired but awake, and I am
so very happy.

For the next eight months, Susan and her fiancé grew
closer together as they prepared for marriage. Susan returned to the city where she taught, put her house up for
sale, and waited anxiously for the school year to end.
On March 16, Susan sold her home. That same day her
fiancé came to visit, and they spent almost a week together.
Then they were apart again, and it was a lonely three
months until she was able to complete her teaching contract
and return home. Meanwhile, her feelings about her im-
pending death would not go away. On May 3, she recorded:

What will I be remembered for here? Have I done
what I've been called to do? What's expected of me
in this extended time? Mom and Dad, please give
heed to my testimony. I love you.

Several months passed, the summer went well, and before Susan knew it, she found herself facing a rapidly ap-
proaching marriage date. She found employment in her
hometown, she and her fiancé chose colors for their wed-
ding, and at last they found a place for their home.
However, as October began, something seemed to go
wrong. Susan's fiancé seemed a little distant, and though she
searched herself for a reason, none came. Susan resolved
that it was her problem and that she would do her best to be
happy. Further, she determined to make her fiancé happy as
well, and on October 19 she recorded her determinations
and her love for the man she was going to marry.
That entry was to be her last.
On October 23, 1982, Susan and her fiancé went out to
dinner, visited with friends, had a bit of a spat, and left to resolve it. Five days later Susan's body was found in the trunk

of her car, which had been hidden on the bank of the river several miles from her home. She had been beaten over the head with a pop bottle, and the broken edge of the bottle had then been used to take her life.

Two years and eleven months had elapsed since Susan's trip to the Cardston Temple, almost exactly three years had passed since the Lord had first given Susan her prophetic dream. And yes, her death began with the brutal blows to her head.

Shortly thereafter Susan's fiancé was charged with the murder, and two years later he was convicted of that murder and was sentenced to 100 years in prison.

It took Susan's parents six months after her passing to locate and then read her journals. Her testimony, so poignantly written and so often expressed, touched their spirits, and within hours they were visiting with their bishop. He gave them a plan of progress, which they followed with exactness, and they have now been sealed in the temple for all eternity.

As we visited recently with Susan's parents, they expressed their sorrow over the events surrounding Susan's death, and their urgent desire to share them. Susan is missed now as much as ever, and for Susan's mother, especially, the pain does not go away. Still, life must go on, they are working to forgive, and Susan's fervent testimony, left for her parents in the pages of her journal, has now become their own.

Truly Susan lived her last years as a disciple of Christ. She stood as a barrier to pain and misery as she protected her parents from her understanding of her own future, and she brought them joy with her lovely and oft-repeated testimony. The ripples for good, caused by the splashing of her righteous life so faithfully recorded in her several journals, will spread out and bless others for generations yet to come. Yes, that is true discipleship indeed.

CHAPTER SEVEN

THAT GLORIOUS GIFT

In October of 1985, Blaine recorded the following entry in his rather sporadically kept journal:

> It is interesting how the shower affects me. I have more ideas and more thoughts that bring understanding when I am taking a shower than at any other time. Strange but true. Such was my experience today.
>
> For several days (and months) I have been contemplating the rather unusual trial Brent and I have been going through this past year. In terms of difficulty, on a scale of one to ten, I would rate it about a ninety-seven. But I have discussed it before in this journal, detailing both the hard things and the remarkable blessings that have come forth from them, and so I won't go into such detail again.
>
> Anyway, for the past several days I have been especially concerned that I be able to correctly understand the ramifications of this very important time. I know that the Lord allows all things to turn to good for them that walk uprightly, and so I have been focusing on that "uprightly" part of the promise, falling short so frequently and yet feeling more close to Heavenly Father than I think I ever have before.
>
> Lately I have prayed more constantly, thought more on the peaceable things of God, tried harder to be a better father and husband, tried harder to assume my patriarchal duties with my brothers and sisters, tried harder to be in tune with the Spirit when I speak to various groups, and so on.
>
> The motivation to do these things, in and of itself,

makes this rather ragged experience worthwhile. More significant, however, has been my increased understanding of the goodness and bounteous love of God for his children, myself and my family included. That has been truly overwhelming.

Beyond all of these, I am certain that there are even greater blessings ahead if I can only prove worthy of them.

The one other thing I have done, motivated by this, is to search the experience in my mind, trying to find other, additional lessons that Heavenly Father might want me to learn.

That searching led to today.

I was standing in the shower this morning reviewing our experience, having a prayer in my heart as I did so (as Alma taught us to do in Alma 34:27 and which admonition I obey only occasionally), when it seemed that my mind was opened for an instant and an understanding was given me that I had never before considered. As Brent once described it (quoting D&C 121), the thought felt like a doctrine of the priesthood, distilling upon my soul as the dews from heaven.

This is the thought: An understanding of the love and mission and sacrifice of Jesus Christ enables a person to correctly interpret mortal experiences, and to translate them into eternal values. These, through application and practice, become celestial characteristics, and thus *we* become celestial.

Translated, we as Latter-day Saints should have remarkable insight into the purposes of our day-to-day experiences, and we should *never* consider them to be mere whims of chance. Because we understand Christ's love, manifested by his teachings and his incredibly selfless act of atonement, we should know our own possible destiny, and we should know that God allows us to have these experiences so that we will be able to fulfill that destiny.

All this understanding came about, of course, through Joseph Smith's first vision and the subsequent revelations given to him and all our other prophets, information that the world simply does not have.

Through those great, divinely appointed prophetic sources, we learn these things, among others:

1. Death is but a step and not an end.

2. It is necessary to undergo lessons that make us more God-like, especially those that are painful and soul-stretching in nature.

3. *All* things work together for good to them that walk uprightly, and to the sanctification of the Church (that is, in making the Church a pure and holy vehicle for declaring the gospel).

4. God's love for man and his amazing reason for creating us is to bring about our immortality and eternal life.

5. Pure love for our fellowmen is what is finally and ultimately required from us if we are to become God-like.

6. We must come to grips with how we feel about our Lord and Savior Jesus Christ, and we learn whether or not those feelings will alter and subdue the carnal nature of our lives so that we may become as he is.

In this concluding chapter, we would like to discuss that last item: how we feel about our Savior. Further, we should like to discuss his mission and show how an understanding of that mission could influence our lives. Let us introduce these thoughts with this painful but beautiful story.

I slipped down beside my hospital bed, my stomach churning—my bishop said I needed to pray for my father, and I was trying. But the words were sticking inside of me, deep down behind all the years of pain and suffering and silence. Now the silence was being broken, and me with it.

How could I pray for my father when the very forming of the words in my mind caused my stomach to convulse. I hated him—vehemently—with the same intensity that my love had once held. And the hatred was tearing me apart.

I climbed back into bed, trembling. I could hear a nurse making her rounds with the tranquilizers. Drizzly rain fell outside. And all I wanted to do was to find some quiet corridor within my mind where I could hide from all the pain.

"Pray for your father," the bishop had said. And

then, "You need to be able to forgive him." Here I was a grown woman with children at home to rear. And yet I lay in a hospital bed, immobilized by fears from my own childhood, struggling through therapy sessions to release the emotional cancer that was twisting itself within me.

Forgive? I didn't know how to forgive. Too much had happened—too much that was beyond forgiveness.

I share this story, not to sensationalize my experience, but because I sincerely pray it might bring hope to others, who, like me, have been victims of incest.

I grew up in the Church. When I was four my father was called to a significant leadership position in our ward. When I was five, he introduced me to sex. Later, repentant and remorseful, he told my mother the terrible thing that had happened. She spoke with me, telling me we would never let it happen again. But it did.

The next recollection I have of such an experience, I told my father I would scream for help if he didn't stop. He put his hand over my mouth and nose until I was fighting for air and said that if I screamed he'd smother me.

And so it was. My younger years were a nightmare. Like a patchwork quilt, memories of perversion were woven among the happy memories. Good things happened, and then something would snap inside my father's mind, and either I or one of my sisters would pay the price.

My mother did not know how to respond. She did not know where to turn for help. I think she was afraid of my father, and she was terribly ashamed of what was happening.

When I was nine, my father asked me to forgive him. "I must have been crazy," he told me. There had been a Church court, but all I knew of it was that one night mother called all of us children together to pray for our father. Then, within a few days, we moved to a new community to start our lives over.

But the nightmare continued. By then I knew my father was not mentally stable. He struggled against whatever possessed him, but again and again he lost the battle. My sisters and I made a promise to protect each other, to never let one of us be alone in a room with him. And that continued to be our major protection until we grew up and moved away from home. He wouldn't do anything if anyone else was watching.

When I was a senior in high school, my elder sister and I shared our father's problem with our bishop, and soon afterward another Church court was held. This time our father was excommunicated. Still, nothing changed in our home except that our mother stopped attending church in a futile attempt to support our father.

I sat down one Sunday next to a girl in my Laurel class, and she asked why my father had been excommunicated. I don't remember what I told her, but after that I started finding excuses for not attending church. I felt I wasn't as good as the rest of the kids in the ward. I'd watch my friends with their fathers and wonder why my family couldn't be like theirs. I was terribly ashamed and hurt over what had happened. It seemed that everyone in the Church knew something was wrong in our home, but I had no one to turn to, no one to share what was happening inside me.

About that time I met a fellow, and we began dating. He wasn't a member of the Church, but by then that didn't seem to matter. With another couple, we spent a lot of time together doing things we shouldn't have. They all drank; I didn't, but I was more comfortable with them than with the LDS kids who now seemed so far above me. It was like a hardness wrapped itself around me, and I began losing my way.

That fall I moved in with a friend, tired of the struggles at home and just wanting to be free. My father was so angry with me he forbade my family to talk to me or see me.

One afternoon a police officer arrived at my apartment, asking to see me. He told me that if I'd testify in a court of law as to what had happened to me and my sisters, he'd see that my father was put away for a long time. But the officer had no idea how much that frightened me, for all I could think of was my father's temper and my past experiences with him. I had memories of one summer day three years before when I'd finally built up enough courage to let him know I'd had enough. I was alone in the bathroom, drawing water for my mother's bath. He came in and tried to take advantage of the situation. I looked him square in the eyes, took his hand from me, and said, "Cut it out." He hit me hard across the face. I ran to mother, and he took up the rest of the fight with her. She was eight months pregnant, and I thought he was going to kill her. My brothers and sisters and I listened outside the door, pleading on our knees that Mother would be safe. After what seemed an eternity, they both came out.

My father left for several days, but the horror of that experience left an indelible imprint upon my mind. I couldn't put my mother in danger again, so I told the officer that I wouldn't testify. He was disappointed but said that if I ever changed my mind to let him know. But I was too afraid to change my mind.

I got married much too young. The marriage lasted only three years, and due to a great deal of physical abuse I finally left my husband. And in the futility of that failure, I began feeling that Heavenly

Father had turned his back on me. "If you're up there," I finally screamed one day, "how could you let all this happen?" But I didn't listen for an answer; I was too hurt to do so, and I moved further away from the truth.

Now, from a hospital bed, I was supposed to pray for my father? I was supposed to forgive the monstrous figure in my life who had terrorized my dreams and perverted so much that was good. My feelings were so confused! I knew hatred wasn't right, but I didn't know how to forgive.

I turned over in my bed and looked at the half-light outside my window. There were bars of a sort outside the glass, and I thought ruefully, "Who'd ever want to get out of here? At least here I'm safe. At least here no one can hurt me." I stared until the window became a blur and my memories became my reality.

After remarrying and finding a measure of happiness, I remembered, the problems my younger sisters were still having gave me courage to do something. On and off they would come to live with us when things were too difficult at home. Then one day, while I was talking to my youngest sister on the phone, she said something that prompted me to call the state attorney general. We made trips back and forth to his office, but in the final analysis nothing could be done. Mother wouldn't sign papers to have Dad committed, fearing what he might do when he was released. What had happened most recently wasn't of a severe enough nature to be acted upon legally. And the statute of limitations had run out on the things that had happened earlier. So there was nothing we could do.

Not too long after that I had a nervous breakdown. It happened after my second child was born. I was in and out of hospitals for two years, and I lived on tranquilizers and from one psychiatric

141

appointment to the next. I suppose it had to happen. Before then, I wouldn't let myself face what I was really feeling—the anger, the hatred, and even the fear. With counseling, I began looking at what had happened in my life rather than trying to hide it. But it was such a terribly painful process to pass through. My children were neglected, my marriage suffered, and I almost lost my husband.

Then I discovered Spencer W. Kimball's *The Miracle of Forgiveness*, at which time a change began taking place in my life. My testimony was being reborn. I could feel the Spirit recalling to my mind things I needed to repent of. And I began earnestly working my way back, reading the scriptures, seeking forgiveness for what I had done that was wrong. But even then, hard as I would try, I couldn't forgive my father. I would see men who reminded me of him, and I would begin shaking. I feared the dark. Sometimes when I was alone, I could hear his laughter. It wasn't happy laughter, either. It was evil—as I had come to visualize him.

Finally I was released from the hospital for the last time, but neither my husband nor I knew how to deal with the intense emotions I was experiencing, as well as the severe, immobilizing depressions. I would awaken in the morning feeling good, and then by evening I would be almost suicidal. Thank goodness for the scriptures! I found insight in Alma 34:34, which says, "That same spirit which doth possess your bodies at the time that ye go out of this life, that same spirit will have power to possess your body in that eternal world."

I knew I didn't want the spirit of suicide with me in the eternal world, and so I kept praying and opening more to the guidance of the Spirit. But, for me, it was a long and rocky road.

Then a miracle occurred. My father became very ill, bedridden, and several times nearly died. At the same time I was prompted to study and learn more of the Savior. The storybook figure I had learned of in my Sunday School classes was to become more to me than a character within the pages of a book. He was to become vital and real in the drama that had been playing itself out in the fragmented pieces of my mind.

I remember one day in early spring. I was shopping for groceries, and as I passed the checkstand, I was drawn very strongly to a book. I purchased it, and when I arrived home, I opened it to a chapter that spoke of the Savior's power to go back with us into the painful memories of the past and heal the small child within us that may have been abused. I thought of my memories and imagined Christ there with me, protecting me from the pain.

At that moment, an incredible catharsis began taking place. I picked up my pen and began writing. Within two days I had recorded every incident in which I had been violated as a child. The experience was more than emotional. It was spiritual and physical to such a magnitude that by the time I had finished writing, my whole soul was wrapped around the bulk of notepaper that contained my story.

Two emotions resulted from this writing. First, as I wrote I felt as if spiritual poisons were being released from my soul. And as the days passed, I began to realize that I was being directed by the Spirit to burn the papers containing my story. And so, responding to these two simultaneous feelings, I burned the papers. I expected with this act to feel a lighter emotional load, but the burden of my feelings for my father was not lifted. The negative feelings were still there, only becoming more intense, until emotional pain became physical pain. It was then that I wondered if I had made a mistake in facing those memories. I felt an imaginary cord wrapping itself around my mind, tighter and tighter, until the pain was so intense I didn't know if I could endure it.

I then asked my husband for a priesthood blessing, during which I was promised mental and emotional rest. I retired to bed and soon fell asleep. Even so, in my dreams the pain increased until I felt I couldn't live another minute with the pressures in my mind. All the bitterness and hatred had exploded, and I couldn't contain it. It was crushing me.

"Please, Father," I heard myself pleading, "if you would do it for Alma, wouldn't you do it for me? If I asked in the name of Jesus Christ, wouldn't you please lift my burden from me?"

Upon this request, my world was transformed into a world that words can't describe. My burden was lifted completely, and an experience too sacred for me to share left me knowing that I needed to accept what was happening and trust in God.

With my prayers finally answered, I wrote my father and informed him that I loved him and that I had completely forgiven him for all the negative experiences of my youth.

And then, six short months later, my father died.

During the funeral services, I listened intently as my father's home teacher described the bitter tears Father had shed during the long months of his illness. While he spoke, my mind reeled as I considered my own struggles and bitter tears that had preceded my moment of forgiveness. "Then," the home teacher concluded, "something changed inside him."

It was then I learned that even though my father had been completely paralyzed and unable to speak, the spiritual change within him had been very obvious to others. The home teacher went on to describe the transformation that he had seen take place in my father's life. He indicated that the tears my father had shed were no longer bitter tears of pain and anguish. Rather, they had a sweetness to them, even a peace—perhaps even a joy.

And as I sat there, I began to realize that in some miraculous way, during the very time when I was experiencing my own healing, my father too had experienced a similar healing within his soul.

Years have passed, and still I remember the power and the sweetness of my experience with the Spirit. In many ways, my father wasted much of his time here on the earth. Certainly he hurt many people. But in the final drama of his life, a miracle occurred, as it did in my own life. The ultimate lesson was simple. No man or woman can heal themselves. That can only be accomplished through the atoning sacrifice of our Lord and Savior Jesus Christ.

Our friend is right. No man or woman can heal themselves, can cleanse themselves from sin and transgression. Cleanliness, being made pure and holy (the Lord's term for this is being sanctified) can come only through the loving gift of our Savior. In the book of Moses, the Lord says:

> I give unto you a commandment, to teach these things freely unto your children, saying: That by reason of transgression cometh the fall, which fall bringeth death, and inasmuch as ye were born into the world by water, and blood, and the spirit, which I have made, and so became of dust a living soul, even so ye must be born again into the kingdom of heaven, of water, and of the Spirit, and be cleansed by blood, even the blood of mine Only Begotten; that ye might be sanctified from all sin, and enjoy the words of eternal life in this world, and eternal life in the world to come, even immortal glory; for by the water ye keep the commandment; by the spirit ye are justified, and by the blood [of Jesus Christ] ye are sanctified. (Moses 6:58-60.)

This is hard doctrine, for to follow it is anything but easy and convenient. To receive this blessing requires an incredible level of dedication and commitment. Yet, if we truly have the testimonies we stand and bear before others, then the price of our discipleship seems low in comparison to the value of the reward. Brother Jeffrey R. Holland says it this way: "Christ has asked demanding and difficult discipleship from the members of his church. He strengthens us for the task and he is patient with our halting efforts, but ultimately—sometime, somewhere—we have to measure up." (*However Long and Hard the Road* [Salt Lake City: Deseret Book, 1985], p. 26.)

Blaine's daughter Tami brought the story quoted below from her philosophy class at BYU. It beautifully clarifies the point we wish to make.

I see the essence of the gospel of Jesus Christ to be a program for perfecting our relationship with other beings. The program is simple, having only two steps. We must learn to love God with *all* our heart, might, mind, and strength. When we are full of that love for him, then he can and will teach us how to love our neighbor as he loves us.

[A crucial point: We cannot know how to love others as our Father loves us without help from him. When we feel love for others and try to help them as we see fit, that is probably a good thing, but it is clearly *not* the pattern of God's love for us. His love for us proceeds out of a perfection of character and an omniscience that no human desire can begin to match. Thus, when we suppose that we can love our neighbor in a godly way by doing what *we* think is best, we are appointing ourselves to be gods, a bit of pride that is hardly justified.]

The gospel gives us a formula for loving God. It is (1) to put our whole faith and trust in Jesus Christ; (2) to repent of all our sins; (3) to make the covenant of baptism under one who has authority from Christ; (4) to receive the Holy Ghost by the laying on of hands of one who has authority from the Savior; (5) to endure to the end in becoming like Christ and knowing him by following the guidance of the Holy Spirit. To love God is to become as he is, and to come to know him is to be one with him.

It is my understanding that there are three basic levels of progress through which the Holy Spirit will lead us into oneness with our Godhead.

The first level is to turn away from being like the world. To this end we are given the Ten Commandments, which are a preparation for joining the Church. If we keep the Ten Commandments, and follow the Holy Spirit by joining the Church, then certain other outward opportunities are given to us, such as keeping the Word of Wisdom, paying tithes and offerings, doing good for others, being active in and filling callings in the Church, and receiving priesthood and the temple ordinances. In all of this we show our love for the Lord, our acceptance of him. Through all of this the Holy Spirit guides us as we humbly seek help in prayer.

The second level is the opportunity to unite with the priesthood authority, which the Savior has placed in his church to help bring us to the Father. He has appointed officers in the Church for the perfecting of the Saints. We cannot grow past the first level until we carefully support, work with, pray for, and love all those whom he, the Savior, has appointed to preside over us in our families and in the Church. To love God is to love his work and the instruments by which he does his work on the earth: his priesthood authorities. Not to love and support them with all of our heart, might, mind, and strength is to reject the Savior who appointed them

147

to preside over us. If we do support them, the Holy Spirit will guide us as we humbly seek help in prayer. (See 1 Samuel 26:7-12.)

When we have found ourselves fully united, in divine love, with the priesthood authority that is over us, then and only then can we go on to the third level, perfection. It is only then that we shall be given the power to perfect every word, every thought, every feeling, every hope, every desire under the tutelage of the Holy Spirit as we seek that help through humble prayer. Then we really do love the Lord with all of our heart, might, mind, and strength. Then we achieve that oneness with the Lord.

If we are able to but do not unite with the priesthood authority the Savior has established on the earth, that is a rejection of the Savior, a declared rejection of love for him. In that condition we cannot keep the first great commandment, which also means that in that condition we cannot keep the second commandment. To pretend to love mankind and to try to make the world a better place while rejecting the Savior and his priesthood authority is a contradiction. Only through the priesthood structure of The Church of Jesus Christ of Latter-day Saints is there any real hope for a righteous means of bringing the misery and woe of mankind to an end and bringing to all men the opportunity of true happiness, love, and accomplishment. (Chauncy C. Riddle, Ph.D., Brigham Young University.)

How and when does this "measuring up" occur? Not, we feel, until our hearts are changed by the power of the Holy Ghost and we understand the magnitude of the price Jesus Christ paid for our cleansing.

In the book of Acts, we read that Saul was traveling on

his way to Damascus to further persecute the Saints of God. Suddenly a light appeared, and he fell to the earth and was introduced to the Lord and Savior Jesus Christ. The trembling and astonished man's first words after that moment were: *"Lord, what wilt thou have me do?"* (Acts 9:6.) On the day of Pentecost, the thousands who through the power of the Holy Ghost had received testimonies of Christ asked Peter the same question: *"Men and brethren, what shall we do?"* (Acts 2:37.)

And always (as is verified in instance after instance throughout the scriptures and in modern times as well), the answers are the same.

Take positive action.

Be baptized.

Receive the Holy Ghost.

Continue in obedience.

Seek the love of God.

Love and serve others.

Five hundred years before the time of Christ, a man named Enos went hunting beasts in the forest. While alone in that setting, the words of the gospel as taught by his father sank deep into his soul, and, finally, wanting desperately the joy his father had spoken of, Enos sank to his knees before the Lord.

All day long he cried out to God in mighty prayer, and when the night came he still raised his voice high to the heavens. Finally God responded: "Enos, thy sins are forgiven thee, and thou shalt be blessed."

Thrilled, Enos asked how his guilt could be so thoroughly swept away.

"Because of thy faith in Christ," God answered, "whom thou hast never before heard nor seen. . . . Wherefore, go to, thy faith hath made thee whole."

Dismissed and probably tired, Enos might well have arisen and gone home to bed. Instead, however, he began again to pray, this time for his family and his friends. On into the night he poured out his soul, struggling in the

Spirit, and finally the voice of the Lord came again, assuring him that the Nephites would be blessed according to how well they kept the commandments.

Once again dismissed, with the first gray light of dawn probably showing in the sky, and with great weariness no doubt upon him, it would surely have been understandable if Enos had arisen and returned to his home and his bed.

But no, he could not! Now he had a pure knowledge of the love and mercy of Jesus Christ, and so, like all others who come to that understanding, Enos cried out, in effect: *"Lord, what wilt thou have me do?"*

Then, under direct inspiration, he prayed for his enemies the Lamanites. Soon he received assurance from the Lord that a record would be preserved for them that they too might be preserved, and from that moment and for the remainder of his life Enos labored to declare the glorious message of the atonement of Jesus Christ. (See Enos 1: 3-26.)

Is that not discipleship? Did not Enos become a barrier to pain and a carrier of joy? Of course. But such discipleship cannot happen, will not happen, until we understand and know of a surety, as did Enos and the others mentioned above, of the mission and power of the Savior.

In other words, we cannot truly become disciples until we know and understand (through divine witness) exactly whom we are disciples to.

Years ago, at Brigham Young University, we asked our students approximately how much time each of them spent each week thinking about Jesus Christ. The hundreds of answers averaged out to 2.3 minutes. This amounts to only 2 hours a year, or only 120 hours in our average, mature lifetime. When we think that we spend only 120 hours out of a possible 525,000 hours considering the Savior, we find ourselves quite shaken. Imagine! The single most important person in their lives was given 2.3 minutes of consideration out of a possible ten thousand and eighty minutes a week. And that 2.3 minutes was usually given at some point during the administration of the sacrament.

Is it any wonder that so many of us struggle with keeping the basic commandments? Is it any wonder that so many of us labor with the higher law of loving ourselves and therefore our neighbors? Is it any wonder that so few among us are effective disciples of Jesus Christ? Is it any wonder that we inflict so much pain upon others, or allow it to be inflicted, when we should be acting as a barrier to it while we are carrying forth joy? Finally, is it any wonder that so many of us seriously question whether or not we will have eternal life?

What is missing, it seems, is the inspired, burning conviction of Christ's divinity and his mission of atonement. In all eternity, only that powerful sort of testimony will bring about our own personal, dedicated response: *"Lord, what wilt thou have me do?"*

Near the end of Jesus' three-year ministry, and at the conclusion of the last supper, Jesus left the city of Jerusalem and led his eleven remaining apostles down across the brook Cedron and up the slope of the Mount of Olives. There, near an olive press called Gethsemane, he left the eleven to wait while he went off to be alone.

What followed we cannot understand, but in some miraculous manner made possible by his innocence, purity, and Godhood, he was able to take upon himself the suffering for our sins.

We know little of this, yet to Joseph Smith the Lord described the experience in this manner: "Which suffering caused myself, even God, the greatest of all, to tremble because of pain, and to bleed at every pore, and to suffer both body and spirit—and would that I might not drink the bitter cup, and shrink—nevertheless, glory be to the Father, and I partook and finished my preparations unto the children of men." (D&C 19:18-19.)

It was so difficult for Jesus, in fact, that when he pleaded that the cup pass from him, God sent an angel to comfort and strengthen him. (Luke 22:43.) It may even have been that the angel placed his hands upon the Savior's head and blessed him with strength to continue.

"No," Father seemed to be saying, "I cannot take this

cup from you. You promised and covenanted to it in the grand council in heaven before the world was, and if I take it away, our entire plan of redemption for mankind will be thwarted. No, my beloved Son, thou must bear this that thou suffereth in patience. But truly the administration and blessing of mine angel will strengthen thee, and if thou bear it well, thou shalt overcome."

In our wildest imaginations we cannot conceive of Jesus Christ shrinking. Yet to him this experience was so horrible that he admits to having done it.

Then he described the shedding of his blood through every pore of his body. Medically this is called hematohidrosis, and it is a usually fatal injury suffered by a very few who have been close to immense concussions, such as bomb explosions, and who have had all the thousands of capillaries in their bodies ruptured. This immense volume of freed blood, having nowhere to go, exits through the sweat glands, and the person bleeds from every pore.

Once this suffering was over, Jesus subjected himself to arrest and was taken before a man named Annas, who was father-in-law of the Jewish high priest Caiaphas. He was questioned, and there is some evidence that Annas's guard beat Jesus in the face with his fist.

From there he was taken to Caiaphas, who called an illegal meeting of the Sanhedrin, the Jewish governing body. These men met throughout the night, with the exhausted Jesus standing before them, while they sought false testimony against him.

At last, near dawn, the testimony was obtained. Caiaphas rent his clothing, judged Jesus a blasphemer, and ordered that he be put to death. But though Caiaphas had the authority to so order, he had no authority to actually execute.

Therefore Jesus was taken before Pilate, Roman procurator in Judea, under the charge of sedition, not at all the same charge as Caiaphas had given him. Pilate questioned Jesus, determined that there was no substance to the charge, received pressure from Caiaphas and many other Jews, and finally deferred the decision to Herod Antipas, tetrarch of Galilee.

Herod was an evil man (he was the only person mentioned in the New Testament as having been called a name by Jesus, who said he was a fox—a scavenger of living and dead flesh). He apparently wanted to see a miracle. He placed his soldiers around Jesus so that they too might observe, and then he commanded Jesus to perform. From what we can tell, Jesus "held his peace."

Angry, Herod ordered his five hundred soldiers to do what they then did, and we have the account of the crown of thorns (not a wreath but an entire cap) being driven onto his head. Then he was given a reed scepter and a royal robe, and one at a time these five hundred men walked past him and slapped him and spat upon him in mockery! That concluded, Jesus was returned to Pilate.

Meanwhile Pilate's wife Claudia had dreamed a dream in which she learned that Jesus was a just man. In fear she pleaded with Pilate that Jesus's life be spared. But Pilate, weak as most men are, could also hear the clamoring for death from his courtyard.

Who knows what motivated him then? Perhaps it was fear of the people; perhaps it was even an attempt to save Jesus' life. Whatever it was, he ordered Jesus stripped and tied to a pillar in public view. Then apparently two soldiers holding flagrums (whips with many strands, each strand tipped with jagged rock or metal or glass) stood behind him, one on either side. At Pilate's order they began what was called scourging, which means removing the flesh. (Scourging was illegal for Romans, and so only Jews and infidels could be so treated. Unfortunately, Jesus was a Jew.)

Some evidence seems to indicate that Jesus was scourged from the base of his neck all the way down to the tops of his ankles, a wracking torture that proved deadly for most who experienced it. Not dying, however, Jesus' bands were loosed and he was held before the people.

"Behold," Pilate told the clamoring crowd (the following dialogue is paraphrased), "this man that we have scourged is

153

Jesus. As today is the eve of your Feast of the Passover, and as it is customary for me to release to you one prisoner on this day, I give you your choice! Will it be Barabbas, the murderer who is finally within our dungeon walls, or will it be this man Jesus, whom I have nearly killed with my scourging?"

Instantly the cry arose. "Release Barabbas! *Crucify* this man!"

Probably both surprised and saddened, but still lacking courage, Pilate called for water and then washed his hands in an ineffectual attempt to rid himself of involvement in the crime.

"Then let his blood be upon you," he stated flatly.

"Wonderful!" the crowd shouted. "Let his blood be upon our heads and upon the heads of our children!"

Jesus was then taken and thrown upon his face in the courtyard. There the beam of the cross was placed upon his shoulders, and amidst whipping and spitting and cursing and kicking, he staggered to his feet. Then, with a brutal shove, he was sent reeling forward among his tormentors.

Jesus was physically exhausted. He had been awake for at least thirty-five hours; he had sweat blood for our sins in Gethsemane; he had been beaten by Annas's guard; he had been forced to stand, bound, all night, while the Sanhedrin considered his case; he had been physically abused by Herod and his men; he had been scourged; and, finally, he had been forced to stagger forward under the weight of the beam of his instrument of execution.

He fell, was whipped to his feet, probably fell again and again, and, finally, outside the gate of Jerusalem, fell once more. This time, no matter how they beat him, he was unable to rise.

Grabbing from the crowd a man, Simon of Cyrene by name, the soldiers put the beam of the cross upon his back and dragged Jesus to his feet, and in that manner they marched both of them to the top of Calvary, also called Golgotha, which is variously translated as "place of death," "place of the skull," or "place of execution."

There Jesus was again stripped and thrown upon his back across the beam; probably one of the soldiers grabbed his hand and yanked his arm straight along the beam. Then he placed his boot upon Christ's hand or arm so that he wouldn't jerk as the monstrous spike severed his large medial nerve.

Ready, another took a large mallet and drove a spike through Jesus' flesh and into the wood. That done, they drove a similar spike through his other hand. Finished, they hoisted the beam into place on the cross and drove a third spike through both of Jesus' feet, fixing them to the cross. Surely, as the scriptures declare, he was wounded for our sins.

Then, with the sign in place proclaiming him king of the Jews, the Romans and the Jews let our Savior hang and writhe and twist in agony, while most of those who watched clapped and mocked and cheered and spit and considered what a great thing it was that they had done.

For about six hours he so suffered, and during that time, according to the witness of Elder Bruce R. McConkie, "all the infinite agonies and merciless pains of Gethsemane recurred." (*A New Witness for the Articles of Faith* [Salt Lake City: Deseret Book, 1985], p. xiv.)

Finally, God the Father, knowing that Christ could not become Savior until he had overcome all things alone, withdrew his Spirit.

In agony such as we cannot contemplate, Jesus then cried out with a loud voice, "Eloi, Eloi, lama sabachthani?" which means, "My God, my God, why hast thou forsaken me?"

And then Jesus endured alone, experiencing all the pain and loneliness and heartache we ourselves feel when we have sinned and the Spirit has withdrawn, when we have lost someone dear and cannot bear to continue alone, when we have caused hurt and pain in others and cannot bear to contemplate the horror of what we have done.

Christ felt these things. He endured them alone! During that eternal time on the cross, he truly felt, and in the feeling he understood. Thus, in a very real way, he is able to give succor and relief to all those who earnestly seek it.

At last, with a cry of joy and relief, he gave up the ghost. And we, two millennia later, spend 2.3 minutes per week considering this and his magnificent teachings.

So in conclusion we ask why? Why did Jesus so suffer? Why did he go through such horror, such incomprehensible pain?

We wonder even yet why he did not die during this terrible time. We think of his suffering in Gethsemane, which would have killed anyone else. We consider his scourging by Pilate, which also could have killed any other man. And finally we think of his six hours on the cross, six hours so filled with agony that it is incomprehensible to think that it could be endured. Yet Jesus Christ suffered all these things and *did not* die!

Why? Because of his godly birthright. Jesus *could not* be killed, for from his conception in his mother's womb he had power over death. (See John 10:17-18.)

Have you ever considered that God the Father gave only one man, Jesus Christ, eternal power over death, and then sent that man here specifically so that he might die? Yet it is true, and therein lies the eternal magnificence of Christ's great sacrifice.

He did it all willingly!

At any point he had the power within himself to withdraw from the events through which he suffered. Think of that! He had the power to quit! Yet even with that power, he chose to do otherwise. He chose to be obedient, he chose to love, both his Father and us his brothers and sisters.

Why? *Because he loved us.* He *loves* us enough to want us to join him and his Father in celestial glory. And how do we do that? By loving him! And according to King Benjamin, that can be done only by loving and serving others.

That and that alone, we testify in all soberness, is how you and we may *become* disciples of our Lord and Savior, Jesus the Christ.

Index

8-11, 113-14; adversely affected by peers, 15-16, 36-37, 43-45, 50-51; abused, 34-35, 57-58, 79-80, 85-87, 138-40; who suffered from divorce, 56-57, 76-78; parents who supported handicapped, 107-10; who felt presence of deceased mother, 125-26

Chirgwin, Jim, 50-51

Christensen, Bernell L., 123-25

Church, date invited to, 73-74

Cleft palate, girl with, 6-7

Competition: theory of, 24-25; effects of, 33-34; within self, 35-36; people who didn't measure up to, 36-39; misconceptions about, 38-42; breeds cruelty and unkindness, 43

Concern. See Kindness, examples of; Love, examples of

Conscience, listening to, 124

Contractor, dishonesty of, 91-93

Cow, sick, anecdote about, 13-14

Coyote, Harold Gos, 24-25

Cruelty, effects of: criticism by children, 15-16, 36-37; parents giving punishment, 18-19, 57-58; mistreatment of handicapped, 22-23, 50-51; rating system, 27-28; physical attacks, 34-35, 57-58, 79-80; perception of being fat, 38-39; constant taunting throughout teen years, 43-45; false reputation, 47-48; child victims of incest, 85-87, 138-40; effects of incest extends to adulthood, 87-89; 137-38, 140-45; spouse abuse, 89-90, 140. See also Unkindness, effects of

Crucifixion, 153-56

Death: woman who anticipated her, 129-34; power over, 156. See also Spirit world

Destruction. See Cruelty, effects of

Deutch's Law: positive side of, 3-7, 11-15; negative side of, 15-19; ripple effect is ramification of, 56

Disbelief, 121-23

Discipleship: mother teaches daughter about, 1-3, 5; loving others is element of, 7-8, 19-21, 41, 55, 156; results of failure in, 15-18; farmer as example of, 69-70; three young people as examples of, 70-74; repentance necessary for, 76; frequently hospitalized man as example of, 114-16; spirituality as element of, 120, 123; of woman who anticipated death, 129-34; loving God is element of, 146-48; through knowledge of Savior, 150-51. See also Love, examples of

Dishonesty, 91-95

Divorce, effects of, 56-57, 76-78

"Dog," student rated as, 27-28

Down's syndrome, accepting child with, 109-10

Ellis, Elaine, 117-18

Ellis, Len, 116-18

Enos, 149-50

Envy, effects of, 28, 38-40

Fasting, youths involved in, 100-101

Father: who beat son, 18-19, 57-58; who victimized family because of immorality, 76-80, 137-45; who nearly died, 96-99; disabled, 110-11. See also Parents

Fatness, girl who suffered from, 38-39

Fighting, sister who was victim of, 34-35

Forgiveness: of God, 47-48, 101-4; peers who do not exercise, 47-48; effects of abuse on, 79-80, 85-89, 137-42; family who lost home exercises, 91-93; of self, 102-3; abused woman finally achieves, 142-45

Friends, making, 70-71

invites date to church, 73-74;
concern for family with retarded
child, 108-9; daughter takes care
of disabled father, 110-11; father
tends man unable to recognize
him, 111-12; couple befriends
immigrant couple, 116-18; Enos
prays for others, 149-50
Knowledge of Latter-day Saints,
136-37

Laurel advisor who helped person
weather crisis, 76-78
Leadership: examples of good, 12-13,
19-21, 100-104, 112, 114-18;
examples of poor, 46, 96-100
Liars. *See* Dishonesty
Life, review of entire, 53-55
Lifting up of others, 49-51
List of things to do as wife, 31-33
Loneliness, effects of, 17, 40-41
Love: parents must teach children
about, 7-8; growing up in atmosphere of, 8-11; effects of, 19-21;
counteracts effects of competition,
48-51; as test of spirituality, 124;
of Jesus Christ, 136, 156; learning
about, 136-37; for God, 146-48
Love, examples of: mother cleans
daughter's room, 1-2; parents
sacrifice for grown children, 3-5;
mother's care and esteem affect
daughter, 5; parents answer
daughter's prayer, 6-7; family
adopts two Brazilian children, 8-9;
boys adopted by foster family,
10-11; Sunday School teachers
who cared, 12-13; neighbors show
concern for boy and sick cow,
13-14; father who repented of
conduct toward son, 18-19;
memories of Wulf Wulfenstein,
19-21; person with muscular
dystrophy, 61-62; teen who
received mirror, 62-65; professor
who bought shoes, 65-66; farmer

who helps neighbors and relatives,
68-70; student who made friends
easily, 70-71; younger athlete
befriended by older athlete, 71-73;
stake president loves youth,
100-101; love brings couple into
Church, 101-4; families with
retarded children, 108-9; daughter
takes care of disabled father,
110-11; father tends man unable
to recognize him, 111-12; family
sells home to help rebellious son,
113-14; love brings immigrant
couple back to Church, 116-18;
love through forgiveness, 144-45;
Enos prays for others, 149-50;
atonement and crucifixion of
Christ, 151-56
Lustfulness, effects of, 26-27. *See also*
Immorality

Manuscript, Book of Mormon, 48
Marriage, experience of second,
125-26
Maternal deprivation syndrome, 8-9
Maxwell, Neal A., 106
McConkie, Bruce R., 155
McKay, David O., 126
Meier, Robert, 37-41
Mirror, gift of, 62-65
Misery, causes of, 15-18, 59-60, 89,
105-6. *See also* Cruelty, examples
of
Missionaries, experience of, 42,
99-100, 125-26
Mother: influence of, 1-3, 5, 11-12;
false expectations for, 29-33; who
ran for public office, 58; who
couldn't protect daughters,
138-41. *See also* Parents
Motivations for competitiveness,
38-40
Murder, premonitions of, 129-34
Muscular dystrophy, persons with,
61-62

Nibley, Hugh, 94-95